The Supreme Court Explained

Also by Ellen Greenberg

The House and Senate Explained: The People's Guide to Congress

The
Supreme
Court
EXPLAINED

ELLEN GREENBERG

W. W. NORTON & COMPANY
New York   London

To Jerome Greenberg,
with love and thanks for all those Johnson's Spoons

Copyright © 1997 by Ellen Greenberg
Cartoons © 1997 by Sidney Harris

All rights reserved
Printed in the United States of America
First Edition

For information about permission to reproduce selections from this book,
write to Permissions, W. W. Norton & Company, Inc., 500 Fifth Avenue,
New York, NY 10110.

The text of this book is composed in Bembo
with the display set in Snell Roundhand
Composition by PennSet, Inc.
Manufacturing by Quebecor Printing Book Group

Library of Congress Cataloging-in-Publication Data
Greenberg, Ellen.
   The Supreme Court explained / Ellen Greenberg.
      p.   cm.
   Includes index.
   ISBN 0-393-04097-6.—**ISBN 0-393-31638-6 (pbk.)**
   1. United States. Supreme Court—Popular works.   2. United
States—Constitutional law—Popular works.   I. Title.
KF8742.Z9G728   1997
347.73'26—dc21   96-39582
                                                                      CIP

W. W. Norton & Company, Inc., 500 Fifth Avenue,
New York, N.Y. 10110   http://www.wwnorton.com

W. W. Norton & Company Ltd., 10 Coptic Street,
London WC1A 1PU

1   2   3   4   5   6   7   8   9   0

Contents

Introduction

"MAYBE HE HAS THE KEY."

The judicial Power of the United States, shall be vested in one supreme Court, and in such inferior Courts as the Congress may from time to time ordain and establish.
—Article III, section 1, of the Constitution of the United States

The Supreme Court of the United States was created by authority of the Judiciary Act of September 24, 1789. It was organized on February 2, 1790, and handed down its first opinion in 1792.

Most of what the Supreme Court does—and it's quite a lot—is done in secret. Approximately seven thousand cases arrive at the Court in the course of a term and, in addition, some twelve hundred applications of various kinds are filed that can be acted upon by a single justice.

Considering that the Court is a public body, one might think that we should be able to see how it makes decisions. But on second thought it becomes apparent that it is important for the Court to work with as little outside pressure as possible. One way to avoid pressure is to keep a low profile.

Supreme Court decisions affect every facet of our lives. The Court not only settles disputes between parties, but its interpretations of the law set the paths that lower courts follow.

This book is about the process by which the Supreme Court goes about its business. It's not about specific cases, though some are mentioned for illustrative purposes; but it's about the inner workings of the Supreme Court—how the justices go about their business.

Perhaps one day the Court will allow the TV cameras of C-SPAN, the cable TV industry cooperative that provides gavel-to-gavel coverage of the House and Senate, or Court TV into its courtroom. Until such time, if you can't get to Washington, D.C., Chapter 1, "The Stage and the Players," will show you what the courtroom looks like and explain who the people are who function within it.

Chapter 2, "The Script—The Words You Hear and What They Mean," is the major portion of the book. If you want to know what "riding circuit" really means, what is meant by a "class action," or how the Fourteenth Amendment to the Constitution guarantees you equal protection under the law, here's the place to look.

The Supreme Court doesn't initiate a case, but individuals, companies, or states can. The third chapter, "The Route to the Supreme Court," explains the Court's jurisdiction and the routes through either the federal or state courts that a case must take to reach it.

Even after a case reaches the Court, it's up to the Court to decide if they will hear it. Chapter 4, "From Intro-

The Supreme Court Explained

The Stage and the Players

"HE'S RIGHT. YOU SIT IN THE NEXT CHAIR BECAUSE I ALWAYS SIT TO YOUR RIGHT, <u>THREE</u> SEATS FROM THE END."

THE STAGE—The Places and
Things You See
See diagram page 2.

a. Marble Columns: In all, twenty-four columns made of Italian marble surround the chamber.

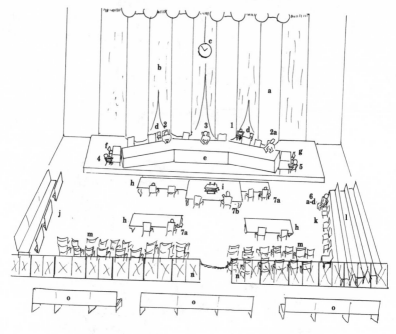

The Stage

a Marble Columns
b Red Drape
c Clock
d Aides' Chairs
e Bench
f Clerk of the Court's Desk
g Marshal of the Court's Desks
h Attorneys' Tables
i Lectern
j Press Section
k Reserved Seating
l Guest Section
m Seating for the Supreme Court Bar
n Bronze Rail
o Visitor's Section

The Players

1 Aides
2 Associate Justices
2a Most Junior Associate Justice
3 Chief Justice
4 Clerk of the Court
5 Marshal of the Court
6a Reporter of Decisions
6b Librarian
6c Law Clerks
6d Retired Justices
7a Attorneys
7b U.S. Solicitor General

b. Red Drape: Justices enter the courtroom through three entrances located behind the drape. The chief justice and two senior associate justices enter through the center, and three associate justices enter through each side.

c. Clock: Large clocks are suspended from the ceiling at both ends of the courtroom.

d. Aides' Chairs: Located behind the justices, the place where aides sit.

e. Bench: The raised mahogany "table" behind which the justices sit. Its wing-shape makes it easier for the justices to see and hear one another.

At each justice's feet is an ornate brass spittoon. A necessity when chewing tobacco was prevalent, all have been converted into wastebaskets. At each place is a pewter drinking cup.

f. Clerk of the Court's Desks: They're used by the clerk or one of his staff.

g. Marshal of the Court's Desks: They're used by the marshal or one of his staff.

h. Attorneys' Tables: Four counsel tables used by lawyers presenting oral arguments. As a reminder of how things used to be, white quill pens are at each place and may be taken as a memento of a lawyer's time before the Supreme Court.

i. Lectern: Lawyers presenting their arguments stand at the lectern. It has a hand crank to adjust its height, and lights to indicate how much time an attorney has left to present his argument. (When a white light goes on, the attorney has five minutes left; when the red goes on, his time has expired.)

j. Press Section: Red upholstered benches located on the left side of the courtroom, they are reserved for members of the Supreme Court press corps.

k. Reserved Seating: Black chairs located on the right side of the courtroom, they are reserved for the justices' law clerks, retired justices, and officers of the Court, for example, the reporter of decisions and the librarian.

l. Guest Section: Red upholstered benches reserved for special guests of the Court. As always with the justices, seniority counts. Guests are seated in order of the seniority of the justice who invited them.

m. Seating for the Supreme Court Bar: Chairs reserved for any member of the Supreme Court Bar who chooses to attend an oral argument.

n. Bronze Rail: It tops grillwork that separates the visitor's section from the courtroom section.

o. Visitor's Section: Oral arguments are open to the public, but seating is on a first-come, first-served basis and there are only 188 seats. (See Chapter 5 for more on visiting the Court.)

THE PLAYERS—The People You
See and Hear
See diagram page 2.

1. Aides: The Court's gofers, four of whom are seated behind the justices when the Court is in session. There are nine chambers aides (one for each justice) and fifteen marshal's aides (including a career supervisor and assistant supervisor). All are hired by the marshal, and justices select their aides from among the general pool. Aides usually work at the Court for two or three years following college graduation. Among other things, they run errands, deliver mail, and help set up the courtroom before Court convenes. During open sessions, they run the audio system and help with seating. They may be asked to pass messages among the justices, to get a needed book from the library or a copy of *United States Reports* (the official, bound Supreme Court compilation of cases; for quick reference, an entire set is kept in an alcove behind the bench).

2. Associate Justices: They sit on either side of the chief justice, alternating from left to right in order of seniority. The most junior associate justice (**2a**) sits on the far right. All associate justices are created equal; that is, each has one vote on any issue. They do, however, vote and speak in order of seniority.

The number of justices is fixed by Congress and has remained at nine (eight associate justices plus a chief justice) ever since passage of the Judiciary Act of 1869. (The original Court had five associate justices and a chief justice. From 1801 to 1869 Congress altered the number of associate justices seven times.) Justices are nominated by the president and appointed with the advice and consent of the Senate.

Each justice is assigned to one or more of the federal appeals courts. Supreme Court justices don't actually sit on these courts but are available to stay an execution, grant bail, or issue injunctions for applicants to the circuits to which they are assigned. Should a justice deny to do as he's asked, the applicant may then apply to another justice.

3. Chief Justice: He is nominated by the president and appointed with the advice and consent of the Senate, and he may or may not be a member of the Supreme Court at the time of his nomination. As with any associate justice, there is no limit to the chief justice's term—the Constitution states only that justices "hold their Offices during good Behaviour." Like all justices the chief justice may, if he wishes, retire at age seventy after serving for ten years as a federal judge, or at age sixty-five after fifteen years' service. To help ensure the judiciary's independence, the Constitution also states that justices "shall, at stated Times, receive for their Services, a Compensation, which shall not be diminished during their Continuance in Office."

Like any associate justice, the chief justice is assigned to one or more of the federal appeals courts. And, like any associate justice, he has only one vote. But that's where the similarity ends; the chief justice's power and authority far surpass that of any associate justice.

The chief justice presides over the Court, is head of the federal judiciary, and during an impeachment trial of a president presides over the Senate. He is permanent chairman of the Judicial Conference of the United States, the body that looks after the administration of the federal judicial system as a whole. And he is also permanent chairman of the Federal Judicial Center's governing board. He is third in protocol (behind the president and vice president) in receiving ambassadors and visiting dignitaries as an official representative of the U.S. government.

Among other things the chief justice may temporarily reassign circuit court judges and set the hours of the Supreme Court's library. He is manager of the Supreme Court Building and chancellor of the Smithsonian Institution.

But perhaps most important, he presides over Supreme Court conferences and in so doing he may direct their discussions. He prepares the initial "discuss" list, the list of cases that the Court will actually consider. His authority is most evident in the assigning of cases for written opinions. If he is on the side of the majority, he will choose the justice who will write the opinion. By so doing he can be assured of its content, style, and slant. By choosing to write an important opinion himself, he may leave his personal stamp on the country's law.

4. Clerk of the Court: His office manages the judicial business of the Court. He receives documents for filing with the Court and has the authority to reject any submissions that don't comply with the Court's rules. He maintains the Court's records and sees to it that they're not removed from the Supreme Court Building without the Court's permission. He's responsible for maintaining the Court's dockets (calendars and agendas) and notifies lower courts of Supreme Court decisions. He also swears in new members of the Supreme Court Bar. During open Court sessions, he and his staff, dressed in morning coats (the cutaways often worn at weddings), use the desks to the left of the bench.

His job is established by statute, and he's appointed by the Court. He oversees a staff of more than twenty.

5. Marshal of the Court: His office manages the operations of the Court. His staff is large and its duties are many. He is in charge of all property of the United States used by the Court or its members—including the Supreme Court Building. His duties include overseeing the Supreme Court Police Force, acting as the Court's paymaster, and looking after visiting dignitaries.

In the courtroom, during public sessions, it's the marshal (or one of his deputies) who, wearing a morning coat, uses the desks to the right of the bench. At 10:00 A.M. on such days, he pounds his gavel and announces: "The Honorable, the Chief Justice, and the Associate Justices of the Supreme Court of the United States." The justices then file into the courtroom and the marshal calls for silence, crying, "Oyez, oyez, oyez [hear ye]." He continues, "All persons having business before the Honorable, the Supreme Court of the United States, are admonished to draw near and give their attention, for the Court is now sitting. God save the United States and this Honorable Court."

During oral arguments he controls the time and the

white and red lights that warn lawyers that their time for oral arguments is about to run out.

The office is established by statute, and the marshal is appointed by the Court, who sets his salary and may remove him from office if it sees fit.

6a. Reporter of Decisions: He and his staff see to the editing of the Court's opinions—correct typographical errors and check citations to make sure they are correct. They add the headnotes—summaries of the cases, and the lineups (who voted how)—to each opinion. They supervise the printing and publication of the Court's opinions —choosing the quality and size of the paper, the type, and the format. And they make sure the first copies get to the Government Printing Office and are published in *United States Reports*.

The reporter of decisions' job is established by statute, and he's appointed by the Court and is subject to removal by the Court.

6b. Librarian: The person appointed by the Court to manage the Court's library. The librarian's post is established by statute, which mandates that he "selects and acquires by purchase, gift, bequest or exchange, such books, pamphlets, periodicals, microfilm and other processed copy as may be required by the Court for its official use and for the reasonable needs of the bar."

The library, located in the Supreme Court Building, is available for use by Court personnel, members of the Bar of the Supreme Court, members of Congress and their legal staffs, and attorneys for the United States and for federal departments and agencies.

6c. Law Clerks: Legal assistants who are generally top-of-their-class graduates of the country's major law schools. Many have clerked previously for a federal judge on a lower court. They come to work for a Supreme Court justice for one year, although some do stay longer.

Each justice can hire up to four clerks. What a clerk does depends on what the justice he works for requires. Some do only research while others may actually write the first draft of their justice's opinions. Most write summaries of certiorari petitions (requests that the Court review a case) and prepare memoranda analyzing cases the Court has undertaken to review.

6d. Retired Justices: They are provided with offices and secretarial help, as well as special seats in the courtroom.

7a. Attorneys: Only lawyers who have been admitted to the Bar of the Supreme Court may argue before it. The rule for admission says that applicants (1) must be admitted to practice law before the highest court of a state, commonwealth, territory, or possession or the District of Columbia for at least three years and (2) that they "must appear to the Court to be of good moral and professional character." Applications for admittance to the Bar are examined by the clerk of the Court's office. The applicant must sign an oath swearing (or affirming) that he will conduct himself "uprightly and according to law" and that he'll support the U.S. Constitution, and he must pay a fee of $100.

An attorney who does not meet the requirement of (1) above but is otherwise eligible for admission to the Supreme Court Bar may be permitted to argue his case *pro hac vice*—"for this one particular occasion." Attorneys qualified to practice in the courts of a foreign country may also be permitted to argue pro hac vice.

On the day they are to appear for oral argument, attorneys are briefed by the clerk of the Court on matters of procedure. They are, for example, reminded that a Supreme Court justice is never to be addressed as "judge."

7b. U.S. Solicitor General: He or a member of his staff represents the U.S. government in cases before the Supreme Court. He decides what cases the government should ask the Supreme Court to review and what position the government should take in cases it brings before the Court. He supervises the preparation of the government's Supreme Court briefs and other legal documents, as well as the conduct of the oral arguments in the Court.

Appointed by the president, he is part of the Department of Justice. He has two offices: one at the Justice Department and the other in the Supreme Court Building.

Like the clerk of the Court and the marshal, the solicitor general and the attorneys for the solicitor general's office still come before the Court wearing morning coats and striped trousers. (At one time all attorneys appearing before the Court dressed this way.)

BEHIND THE SCENES PLAYERS

The Office of Legal Counsel: This office has two attorneys—the Court counsel and the staff counsel—who are appointed by the chief justice to serve as general counsels to the Court. They deal with anything from personal grievances to advising the clerk of the Court on procedural matters. Unlike the justices' law clerks, who serve for only a short time, the counsels serve at least four years.

Chief Justice's Administrative Assistant: He is appointed by the chief justice to help him manage the Court's non-judicial business. Among other things, he and his staff do research and provide supportive analysis for the chief justice's public addresses and statements. They assist in organizing legal conferences and in the task of explaining to the public the role of the Supreme Court and the federal judicial system. The administrative assistant also helps in preparing the Court's budget and in handling personnel matters.

Office of the Curator: He's appointed by the chief justice. When you visit the Supreme Court Building, it's the

The Script

The Words You Hear and What They Mean

"FRANKLY, I SOMETIMES FORGET WHICH IS AN AMENDMENT AND WHICH IS A COMMANDMENT."

A.

Accessory: If you weren't actually there when a crime was committed but helped or encouraged someone in the commission of a criminal offense, you are still a participant in that crime—you're an **accessory before the fact.** If you've covered up a crime or helped the criminal to escape, you're an **accessory after the fact.**

Accomplice: Someone who helps another in the commission of a crime.

Accused: The defendant in a criminal lawsuit. (See also Defendant.)

Acquittal: A court's or jury's decision that a criminal defendant has not been proven guilty beyond a reasonable doubt. If you've been acquitted, you'll be released, and you can't be prosecuted again for the same act.

Adjudicate: To decide a case.

Administrative Office of the United States Courts (AO): The agency that takes care of the nonjudicial, administrative business of the federal courts. For example, it prepares and submits the budget and legislative agenda for the courts to the Judicial Conference, who sends it along to Congress; and it monitors legislation that affects federal court operations and personnel. The AO performs audits (financial examinations of court accounts); and compiles and publishes statistics on the volume and distribution of the business of the courts.

Its director and deputy director are appointed by the chief justice after consultation with the Judicial Conference. The AO is headquartered in Washington, D.C.

Advice and Consent: The Constitution gives the president the power to appoint the justices of the Supreme Court, but there's one catch: the president must have the Senate, after debating the issue, give *its* approval for the appointment. (See Confirmation.)

Affidavit: A written statement that's sworn to before a court officer or a notary public. It's given voluntarily and may be for the benefit of one party; the opposition need not be told about it. (See Deposition.)

Affirm: To agree with. If an appellate court's decision agrees with one reached by the lower court, the lower court's decision is said to be affirmed. (See also Remand; Reverse.)

A Fortiori: Literally, "from the stronger" (argument). To draw a conclusion that because one thing is true another thing must also be true. For example, if you're not guilty of manslaughter because you didn't kill anyone, then a fortiori you're not guilty of murder.

American Bar Association Committee on Federal Judiciary: Set up by the Bar Association to advise the Senate and the president on the qualifications of nominees to the federal courts. It has at times been controversial, since politicians have thought it to favor one political party over another. (President Reagan submitted candidates' names to the committee only after they'd been sent to the Senate.) After investigation by the committee, potential nominees to the Supreme Court are given one of three ratings: well qualified, qualified, not qualified.

Amicus Curiae: Literally, "a friend of the court." A person or group who is not a party to the lawsuit but who has information or experience that is thought will be helpful in deciding the case. They sometimes are parties who will be affected by the outcome of the case. They may be asked by one side or the other to participate or, with permission of the Court, they may join the case on their own initiative.

Answer: The formal, written statement given by a defendant in response to a civil complaint. It also sets out the grounds for his defense, and perhaps counterclaims against the plaintiff.

Appeal: A legal procedure in which a case is brought to a higher court in the hopes that it will review a lower court's decision and overturn it. To make such a request is **to appeal** or **to take an appeal.** For example, a case decided in the District Court of Maryland may be appealed to the United States Court of Appeals for the Fourth Circuit; it may then be appealed to the highest court of appeals, the U.S. Supreme Court. (See Certiorari.)

Appellant: The loser in a lawsuit; the one who's bringing his case to a higher court for review of the lower court's decision. He wants the lower court's decision overturned. (See Appellee.)

Appellate Jurisdiction: See Jurisdiction.

Appellee: The person who won his case in the lower court and is being made to defend it in a higher court where it has been brought on appeal. He wants the lower court's decision to stand. (See Appellant.)

Arraignment: A proceeding in which a person accused of committing a crime is brought into court, told of the charges against him, and asked to plead guilty or not guilty.

B.

Bail: Security in an amount set by a judge (usually in the form of money). It's granted in exchange for the release from legal custody of a criminal defendant or witness to make sure that he'll appear in court on the day and time appointed. If a person doesn't show up at the appointed time, he's said to have "jumped bail," and he forfeits his security.

Bailiff: A court attendant who may serve as a messenger or usher.

Bench Opinion: The first version of a decision. The Court Publications Unit prints 225 copies, about 175 of which go to the Public Information Office for distribution to the press as the opinions are announced in the courtroom. The remaining copies primarily go to the general public and people with a special interest in a case.

Bench Trial: A trial without a jury; one in which a judge decides the case.

Bill of Attainder: A legislative act that inflicts punishment on a person or members of certain groups without first trying them in a court of law. It's forbidden by Article I, section 9, clause 3 of the Constitution.

Bill of Rights: The first ten amendments to the U.S. Constitution. They were added to the Constitution in 1791.

Brethren: Literally, "brothers." The Supreme Court justices are sometimes referred to as "the brethren," despite having two women in their midst. They may address or refer to each other as "my brother" or, if the shoe fits, as "my dissenting brother."

Brief: A written document that a lawyer uses to give the court the facts essential to his case and the legal arguments that support his side. Sometimes a brief will offer a policy argument; that is, it will try to convince the Court that its position is not only good law but good public policy.

The Supreme Court's rules order that briefs "be concise, logically arranged with proper headings, and free of irrelevant, immaterial or scandalous matter." The Court also lays down rules about the way a brief must be presented. For example, a brief written by an amicus curiae (a friend of the court) in support of the plaintiff must be no more than thirty pages and have a light green cover. If the amicus curiae's brief is in support of the defendant, the page limit is the same, but the cover must be dark green.

Burden of Proof: The duty to substantiate the facts that are in dispute. For example, if you're accused of a crime, the burden of proof is on the prosecutor—he has to prove you guilty.

C.

Capital Offense: A crime punishable by death. If someone has been convicted of treason, the U.S. government can call for the death penalty. Bail is not usually permitted for capital offenses.

Case Law: The law that's been handed down in previous court decisions, as opposed, for example, to statutes enacted by a legislature. (See Common Law.)

Certified Order List: See Orders List.

Certiorari, Writ of: Often referred to as "cert." When a party wants its case reviewed, it asks the Supreme Court to direct the lower court to supply the Supreme Court with the records of the case. Most cases come to the Supreme Court via writs of certiorari, but few such cases are actually heard. (See Rule of Four.)

Chambers: A justice's office. At the Supreme Court each justice's chambers consists of his office and the two offices used by his clerks and secretary(s). A private bathroom is also part of the suite. The chief justice's chambers includes the justices' conference room. When an associate justice leaves the Court, the most senior associate justice has the option to take over his suite. If he declines, the next most senior associate justice gets his chance, and so on down the line.

Charge to the Jury: The judge's instructions to the jury concerning the law that applies to the facts of the case being tried.

Chief Judge: The judge who has primary responsibility for the administration of a court, and also decides cases. Chief judges for the district courts and courts of appeals are selected according to seniority. The chief justice of the Supreme Court is appointed by the president with, of course, the advice and consent of the Senate.

Circuit Courts of Appeal: Their name was changed to courts of appeals in 1948. They were originally called circuit courts because the judges traveled from place to place holding court. (See United States Courts of Appeals; Riding Circuit.)

Circumstantial Evidence: Indirect evidence as opposed to direct evidence, which includes eyewitness and scientific evidence, for example, DNA.

Citation: (1) The way a court's decision is identified in the legal literature. Citations tell you the case's name, which court made the decision and in what year, along with the name of the reporter in which the case can be found (see Chapter 6). (2) A summons to appear in a specific court on a specific day.

Civil Law: The part of the law concerned with matters that are other than criminal. (See also Criminal Law.)

Class Action: A lawsuit brought on behalf of all members of a group sharing a common interest. The action may be brought by one or more individuals. Once the class is certified by the court, the results are binding on all members of the class save those who excluded themselves upon receiving notification of the action to be taken. In a class action suit, women sued Dow Corning Corporation, charging that the silicone breast implants the company manufactured caused illness.

Clerk of Court: An officer appointed by the court to work with the chief judge in overseeing the court's administration, especially to assist in managing the flow of cases through the court and to maintain court records. In the Supreme Court the clerk of the Court has much the same duties, along with some special ones, including the swearing in of new members to the Supreme Court Bar.

Code: A collection of laws. For example, the motor vehicle code refers to the laws having to do with automobiles.

Co-defendant: See Defendant.

Comity: Courtesy. Judicial comity isn't a rule of law, it's a rule of convenience by which one court defers to another's jurisdiction. Comity is for nonrequired recognition, for example, recognition of a divorce decree issued by a foreign court. (See also Full Faith and Credit.)

Commerce Clause: The common name given to Article I, section 8, clause 3 of the Constitution. While section 8 covers a wide range of matters—everything from coining money to declaring war—it's clause 3 that gives Congress the power "to regulate Commerce with foreign Nations, and among the several States, and with the Indian Tribes."

In 1824, in *Gibbons v. Ogden*, the court for the first time defined Congress's power over interstate commerce. It ruled that Congress could regulate commerce affecting more than one state, for example, the transportation of both people and things across state lines.

The commerce clause was also the basis for the Court's 8–1 decision in the 1911 case *Standard Oil Co. v. U.S.*, one of the most important antitrust cases. In it the Court laid out the "rule of reason," holding that in accord with the Sherman Antitrust Act only "unreasonable" trusts restrained trade. The decision broke up Standard Oil's monopoly.

Common Law: The legal system that originated in England and is now in use in the United States. It's based on judicial decisions (precedents) rather than legislative action (statutes). Law that has been enacted by a legislature takes precedent over common law. (See Case Law; Precedent.)

Complaint: A written statement by the plaintiff—the person filing the lawsuit—stating the wrongs allegedly committed by the defendant.

Concurring Opinion: An opinion that's in agreement with the result reached by the majority but disagrees with the reasoning that led the majority to its decision. A justice may write a concurring opinion, giving his own reasons for reaching the decision. Other justices may add their names to the concurring opinion. (See also Dissenting Opinion; Majority Opinion.)

Conference: A working meeting of the Supreme Court justices. Conferences are held to decide which cases the Court will review and to consider cases and reach decisions on them. None but the justices attend, and no minutes are kept. By tradition, conferences begin with the justices shaking hands with one another. Because no staff are present, the justice with the least seniority acts as doorkeeper, opening the door to ask for any material the justices may need.

Confirmation: An informal term for the Senate's giving its advice and consent to a presidential nomination, for example, that of a Supreme Court justice.

Consent Decree: A settlement agreement that has been reached by the parties to a lawsuit. Once given the court's okay, it becomes an enforceable order.

Constitution of the United States: Made up of a Preamble, seven articles, and (at present) twenty-seven amendments, it's the document that sets out the principles upon which our republic is governed. Changes to the Constitution must be ratified, approved, by three fourths of the states. State constitutions serve the same purpose for the individual states.

Contempt, Civil and Criminal: If you're guilty of **civil contempt,** you failed to carry out an order of the court that would have benefitted another party to the case. If you're guilty of **criminal contempt,** you've been found to have shown disrespect for the court or to have obstructed its work.

Contract: A legally enforceable agreement between two or more people that creates an obligation to do or not to do a particular thing. For example, a lease is a contract between you and an apartment owner, whereby you get to use his property, providing you pay him a stipulated amount and abide by certain rules. If you haven't kept your end of the bargain, you may be found in **breach of contract.**

Conviction: A judgment of guilt against a criminal defendant.

Counsel: (1) Legal advice. (2) A term used to refer to a lawyer in a case.

Counterclaim: An assertion of a right to money or property that a defendant makes against a plaintiff—the person who brought the lawsuit in the first place.

Court: A government entity whose job it is to resolve legal disputes. Judges sometimes use "court" to refer to themselves in the third person, as in "the court has read the briefs."

Court Packing: The attempt by the president to fill a court with justices who he thinks will carry out his particular vision or agenda. In 1937, President Franklin Roosevelt attempted to reorganize the federal courts. Among other things, he asked that for every justice over the age of seventy who failed to retire, the president have the right to nominate another justice. The president was limited to six such appointments. Roosevelt's attempt to thus "pack" the Court with his appointees failed. You can hear his Fireside Chat on the matter by visiting the Internet (see Chapter 5, "Reaching Out," for the Internet site).

Court Reporter: A person who makes a word-for-word record of what is said in court and produces a transcript of the proceedings upon request. In the Supreme Court it's the marshal or one of his staff who tapes the audio portion of oral arguments.

Courts of Appeals: See United States Courts of Appeals.

Criminal Law: The law that deals with crime, as well as punishment for breaking the law. (See also Civil Law.)

D.

Damages: In civil cases, money paid by defendants to successful plaintiffs to compensate them for their injuries. Not only do you lose the case, you pay for it as well.

Data Systems Office: The office that prints and processes the Supreme Court's documents and electronically transmits the Court's opinions to outside agencies.

Decision Days: Tuesdays and Wednesdays in weeks when oral arguments are heard; Mondays during other weeks. It's the time during which the Court announces its decisions to the public. The justices assemble in the Supreme Court chamber, and the decision is announced by the justice who wrote the Court's opinion. He doesn't have to read the whole opinion; he may summarize it or only state the result. The writers of concurring and dissenting opinions may also state their positions.

Declaratory Judgment: A type of decision handed down by a court. Here the court gives its interpretation of the matter at hand, but doesn't order that the parties in the case take any specific action.

De Facto: Literally, "as a matter of fact." The term is used as a qualifier as, for example, in "de facto segregation." De facto segregation is segregation in Northern cities resulting not from enforced laws, but rather from, among other things, peoples' economic means. (See also De Jure.)

Default Judgment: A decision rendered against a defendant when he fails to answer charges or appear in court.

Defendant: In a civil case, the person against whom a lawsuit is filed; the person being sued. In a criminal case, such a person is referred to as the accused. A **co-defendant** is someone who is linked to one or more defendants in a single lawsuit.

De Jure: Literally, "as a matter of law." A term used as a qualifier, for example, as in "de jure segregation." De jure segregation is segregation that was intended and enforced by law. (See also De Facto.)

Deliberate: To carefully consider, weigh, discuss, and/or examine evidence in order to reach an opinion.

Deposition: An oral statement taken out of court but given under oath. As in a courtroom, it is in question-and-answer format, and the opposing side is allowed to be there, make objections, and cross-examine. Such statements are often taken to examine potential witnesses, to obtain discovery, or to preserve testimony to be used later in trial. (See Discovery.)

Dicta: See Obiter Dictum.

DIG: An acronym for "dismiss certiorari as improvidently granted." The justices may upon further deliberation decide to withdraw their grant of certiorari. In other words, they've changed their minds and won't hear the case. In the Court's jargon they are said to "DIG" the case.

Discovery: After the lawsuit starts, the way one party learns what the other party or nonparties know. Information is most often disclosed through depositions, written interrogatories, or the exchange of documents. The scope of discovery is broad. It's set out in the Federal Rules of Civil Procedure and the Federal Rules of Criminal Procedure; most states follow all or part of these rules.

Discretionary Jurisdiction: A legal power given a court to hear and decide a case, but one the court may or may not choose to exercise.

Discuss List: A list of cases compiled by the chief justice. It's made up of cases sent to the Court for review that he feels should be heard by the Court. He circulates the list to the associate justices, and they may add any cases they wish to it. Only those cases on this special list are discussed in conference. It's a time-saving device that helps keep the Supreme Court's case load down to a manageable size. It's also another example of the chief justice's ability to control the Court.

Dismissal: In a civil case it's the dropping of the lawsuit; in a criminal case it's the dropping of the charges. When a motion is dismissed it means it has been denied. When an appeal is dismissed it means the judgment of the lower court stands.

Dissenting Opinion: An opinion by a justice who disagrees with the majority's decision. He may not produce his own written opinion but may simply declare himself as dissenting.

A dissent can't change the Supreme Court's decision (the Court has already decided the case), but it can influence public opinion. A dissenter may hope that a future Court, rereading his legal reasoning, will overrule the majority opinion. (See Concurring Opinion; Majority Opinion.)

District Courts: See United States District Courts.

Docket: (1) The court's calendar listing the cases the court will be hearing. (2) A log containing brief entries of court proceedings.

Double Jeopardy: See Fifth Amendment.

Due Process: See Fifth Amendment; Fourteenth Amendment.

E.

Eighth Amendment (1791): Part of the Bill of Rights, it states, "Excessive bail shall not be required, nor excessive fines imposed, nor cruel and unusual punishments inflicted."

In 1983, in *Solem v. Helm*, the Court for the first time ruled on the length of a prison sentence in light of the prohibition against cruel and unusual punishment. In a 5–

F.

Federal Judicial Center: Located in the Dolley Madison House in Washington, D.C., it's the judicial branch's agency for planning and policy research, training and development, and continuing education. Its basic policies and activities are determined by its board, which is made up of two judges of the U.S. courts of appeals, three judges of the U.S. district courts, and one bankruptcy court judge. They are all elected for four-year terms by the Judicial Conference of the United States. The director of the Administrative Office of the United States Courts is a permanent member of the board, and the chief justice of the Supreme Court is its permanent chair. The board meets four times a year. See also Appendix A.

Federal Question: Jurisdiction given to federal courts to hear cases involving the interpretation and application of the U.S. Constitution, acts of Congress (federal statutes), and treaties.

Felony: A crime carrying a penalty of more than one year in prison.

Fifth Amendment (1791): It's about grand juries, double jeopardy, self-incrimination, due process, and just compensation. Part of the Bill of Rights, this amendment says: (1) that with some exceptions, an indictment by a grand jury is necessary before you can be tried for a capital or "infamous" crime; (2) that you can't be tried for the same crime twice; (3) that you can't be made to be a witness against yourself; (4) that the government can't deprive you of life, liberty, or property without due process of law; and (5) that if your property is taken from you for public use, you have to receive just compensation.

The Miranda Rule, set out in 1966 by the Supreme Court in its 1966, 5–4 ruling in the case of *Miranda v. Arizona*, dealt with self-incrimination. It requires that before asking any questions, police give suspects "Miranda Warnings," informing them of their right to remain silent (to avoid self-incrimination), that anything they say may be used against them, and that they have the right to counsel under the Sixth Amendment.

File: To place a paper in the official custody of the clerk of the court, which he enters into the records of a case. A lawyer "files" a brief.

First Amendment (1791): It protects freedom of the press, of speech, of religion, and more besides. Part of the Bill of Rights, it states, "Congress shall make no law respecting an establishment of religion, or prohibiting the free exercise thereof; or abridging the freedom of speech, or of the press; or the right of the people peaceably to assemble, and to petition the Government for a redress of grievances."

In 1962, in *Engel v. Vitale*, the Supreme Court in a 6–1 decision based on the establishment clause of this amendment, held that public schools could not require children to recite even a nondenominational prayer.

In 1971, in *N.Y. Times Co. & Washington Post v. U.S.*, which concerned freedom of the press, the Supreme Court in a 6–3 per curiam decision forbade prior restraints and allowed the publication of the Pentagon Papers—articles concerning the country's involvement in Vietnam that were based on classified documents and whose publication the government had sought a court order to bar. (See also Per Curiam.)

Fourteenth Amendment (1868): Referred to as the equal protection clause, it addresses citizens' rights. It guarantees that anyone born or naturalized in the United States is a citizen of the United States and the state in which he lives. It goes on to say: "No state shall make or enforce any law which shall abridge the privileges or immunities of citizens of the United States, nor shall any state deprive any person of life, liberty, or property without due process of law; nor deny any person within its jurisdiction equal protection of the law."

In 1896, in *Plessy v. Ferguson*, by an 8–1 vote the Supreme Court said separate but equal facilities aboard a train did not violate this amendment. In 1954, by a unanimous vote, the Court in *Brown v. Board of Education of Topeka* overruled *Plessy v. Ferguson* and said that the separate but equal doctrine violated the equal protection clause (Article XVI, section 1) because the separate schools were inherently unequal. The Court thus required integration of the public schools.

With *Gideon v. Wainwright* (1963), the Court overturned *Betts v. Brady*. *Betts* had held that the Fourteenth Amendment's due process clause did not mean that states were obliged to supply an attorney to a defendant who couldn't afford his own counsel. In *Gideon* the Court ruled that the Fourteenth Amendment's due process clause did indeed extend to defendants, in both state and federal cases, the right to counsel guaranteed by the Sixth Amendment. Justice Hugo Black had written the dissent in *Betts*; he wrote the unanimous opinion in *Gideon*, overturning it.

Fourth Amendment (1791): Part of the Bill of Rights, this amendment guarantees our right to be secure in our homes and property from unreasonable searches and seizures. The second part of the amendment concerning search warrants states that "no Warrants shall issue, but upon probable cause, supported by Oath or affirmation, and particularly describing the place to be searched, and the persons or things to be seized."

In 1961, in *Mapp v. Ohio*, by a 5–4 vote the Supreme Court said that evidence at both state and federal trials must be *excluded* if it was obtained in violation of this amendment. That's why this amendment is sometimes referred to as the exclusionary clause.

Full Faith and Credit: Article IV, section 1, of the Constitution states, "Full Faith and Credit shall be given in each State to the public Acts, Records, and judicial Proceedings of every other State." In other words, what the courts of one state decide is binding on the courts of another. In situations concerning foreign judgments, full faith and credit does not apply, but comity may.

G.

Grand Jury: A group of people (the number varies from state to state, but it's most often twenty-three) who've been selected to hear evidence against an accused person. If the jury decides (and here the majority rules) that there is enough evidence to warrant it, an indictment (a formal charge) is issued and the accused is held for trial. Grand jury proceedings are not open to the public. (See also Petit Jury.)

H.

Habeas Corpus: A writ that is usually used to bring a prisoner before the court to determine the legality of his imprisonment. If the imprisonment is not justified, the court orders that the prisoner be released. It may also be used to bring a person in custody before the court to give testimony or to be prosecuted. It's also known as **the Great Writ.**

Headnote: See Syllabus.

Hearsay: An out-of-court statement that is offered in court to prove the truth of that statement. Although there are many exceptions, hearsay is usually not admissible as evidence in court. Unless it was your mother's dying declaration, you probably won't be able to repeat it to a judge and jury.

$\mathcal{I}.$

Immunity: When a court exempts you—grants you immunity—you are safe from prosecution. A court usually grants immunity in exchange for a person's giving testimony that it needs in order to gain a conviction. Immunity is often given to a witness whose testimony would lead him to incriminate himself.

Impeach: To charge a federal official, including the president or a Supreme Court justice, with misbehaving in office. The Constitution gives the House of Representatives the power of impeachment, and the Senate the power to try all impeachments. The chief justice of the Supreme Court serves as presiding officer of the Senate during the impeachment trial of a president.

In 1868, Chief Justice Salmon P. Chase presided over the only presidential impeachment trial ever held; the president was Andrew Johnson, and he prevailed. The only justice ever to be brought to trial was Samuel Chase (no relation to Salmon P.), in 1804, and he too prevailed. In 1969, Justice Abe Fortas resigned from the Court when threatened with impeachment.

In Camera: "In chambers." It refers to meetings that are held in a judge's chambers and hence out of view of the public and jury. Such a meeting may be called to examine evidence to decide whether it will be presented to the jury.

Indictment: The formal charge issued by a grand jury stating that there is enough evidence that the defendant committed the crime to justify bringing him to trial; it is used primarily for felonies.

In Forma Pauperis: Literally, "in the manner of a pauper." An appeal may be brought by a person unable to pay the court costs. If his petition is granted, he doesn't have to pay costs nor does he have to adhere to certain of the Supreme Court's rules, for example, the number of copies of a brief that need to be printed. In 1994 there were 4,858 such cases filed.

Information: A formal, written accusation that the defendant committed a misdemeanor. It's brought by a government attorney rather than a grand jury.

Injunction: A court's command to do something (a **mandatory injunction**) or refrain from doing something. A person violating an injunction is in contempt of court and may be fined and/or imprisoned. Injunctions may be **permanent** or **temporary** and are used to prevent irreparable damage or injury.

In Personam: An action directed against a person. (See also In Rem.)

In Re: Literally, "in the matter of." Used in the title of a case when there are no actual opponents. It refers instead to the person who is the primary subject of the case. It's often used in cases involving juvenile offenders. For example, *In re Gault* was a 1967 case involving a fifteen-year-old's right to the same due process protections as an adult. Gault's father sought to get his son released from prison. He brought an action against "the juvenile justice system" (a "thing," not a person or government).

In Rem: An action against a thing, for example, a tax foreclosure proceeding, as opposed to *in personam*, an action directed against a person.

Instructions: A judge's explanation to the jury before it begins deliberations of the questions it must answer and the law governing the case.

Interlocutory Decree: A preliminary order or judgment issued by a court before final adjudication of the matter before it. (See also Injunction.)

Interrogatories: Written questions that one party asks the other. The answers must be written under oath. (See Discovery.)

Interstate Commerce: See Commerce Clause.

Issue: (1) The disputed point in a disagreement between two parties to a lawsuit. (2) To send out officially, as in to issue an order.

J.

Judge: A government official with authority to decide lawsuits brought before courts. (See Justice.)

Judgment: The official decision of a court finally determining the respective rights and claims of the parties to a suit. (See also Opinion.)

Judicial Conference of the United States: The governing body for the administration of the federal judicial system. Functioning as a kind of board of directors, among other things, it may suggest to Congress ways in which federal courts' operations could be improved. It has twenty-seven members—the chief justice of the Supreme Court, the chief judge of each of the thirteen courts of appeals, a district judge elected from each of the twelve regional circuits, and the chief judge of the Court of International Trade. The chief justice of the Supreme Court presides over the conference, which meets twice a year—usually in March and September. It meets in the East Conference Room (one of the two ceremonial conference rooms in the Supreme Court Building).

Judicial Review: The doctrine that states that courts of law have the power to review acts by government officials, entities, and lower courts. Federal and state courts may exercise the power of judicial review, but in matters concerning the U.S. Constitution the Supreme Court has the final word.

In the area of constitutional law, the judiciary has the power to decide whether something another branch of government does is in keeping with the Constitution. The Supreme Court first set this out in 1803 in *Marbury v. Madison*, stating, "[it's] the province and the duty of the judicial department to say what the law is."

The Supreme Court can't give advisory opinions; Congress can't come to the Court and ask it to decide if a bill it *plans to enact* is constitutional. That issue may only be decided *after* the bill becomes a law and is challenged in the courts.

Jurisdiction: (1) The legal power of a court to hear and decide a case. **Concurrent jurisdiction** exists when two courts have the simultaneous ability to hear the same case. (2) The geographic area over which a court has authority to decide cases. For example, the U.S. District Court for the Eastern District of New York may hear a case in Brooklyn but not one in Buffalo. The Supreme Court has nationwide appellate jurisdiction.

The Supreme Court has **original jurisdiction** (no other court need first consider the matter) in cases involving ambassadors from other countries and in suits to which a state of the United States is a party. It has **appellate jurisdiction** in cases brought on appeal from lower federal courts and from state courts when an issue concerning federal law is involved.

Jurisprudence: The study of law and the structure of the legal system.

Jury: People selected according to law and sworn to inquire into and declare a verdict on matters of fact. (See Grand Jury; Petit Jury; Seventh Amendment.)

Justice: A government official with authority to decide lawsuits brought before courts. The title "justice" is commonly given to a judge of an appellate court; that's why the members of the Supreme Court are called justices.

L.

Landmark Decision: A legal decision that marks a turning point in the law, for example, a Supreme Court decision that sets the country in a new direction. *United States v. Nixon* was such a case.

President Nixon refused to give up tapes of conversations between himself and his aides that had been subpoenaed by a special prosecutor looking into the Watergate break-in. Nixon claimed he was shielded by executive privilege and the separation of powers. In 1974, in an 8–0 decision (Justice Rehnquist didn't take part), the Court held that in a criminal trial, unless national security is involved, a president is subject to the same rules as the rest of us.

Lawsuit: A legal action brought by a plaintiff against a defendant. It's based on a complaint that the defendant's failure to perform a legal duty harmed the plaintiff.

LEXIS: Like WESTLAW, LEXIS is a private legal database used by lawyers to aid them in research. It can be searched by key word for specific cases. All Supreme Court decisions are available on LEXIS the same day they are handed down.

Lineup: The information at the end of the syllabus (summary) that appears at the beginning of each Supreme

Court opinion. It tells how each justice voted in the case.

Some lineups are simple. For example, in 1996 in *Neal v. United States*, which dealt with sentencing in a drug case, the lineup reads, "Kennedy, J. ["J." stands for "Justice," "JJ." for "Justices," "C.J." for "Chief Justice"] delivered the opinion for a unanimous Court."

And some are complex; for example, in *McNeil v. Wisconsin*, a self-incrimination case decided in 1991, the lineup reads, "Scalia, J., delivered the opinion of the Court, in which Rehnquist, J., and White, O'Connor, Kennedy, and Souter, JJ., joined. Kennedy, J., filed a concurring opinion. Stevens, J., filed a dissenting opinion, in which Marshall and Blackmun, JJ., joined."

And some are even more complex; for example, in a 1993 case, *Hartford Fire Insurance Co. et al. v. California et al.*, the lineup read this way: "Souter, J., announced the judgment of the Court and delivered the opinion for a unanimous Court with respect to Parts III and IV, in which Rehnquist, C.J., and White, Blackmun, and Stevens, JJ., joined, and an opinion with respect to Part II-B, in which White, Blackmun, and Stevens, JJ., joined. Scalia, J., delivered the opinion of the Court with respect to Part I, in which Rehnquist, C.J., and O'Connor, Kennedy, and Thomas, JJ., joined, and a dissenting opinion with respect to Part II, in which O'Connor, Kennedy, and Thomas, JJ., joined."

Litigants: The people actively involved in a court case; both plaintiffs and defendants.

Litigation: A case, controversy, or lawsuit. (See Litigants.)

Magistrate Judges: Judicial officers who assist U.S. district judges in getting cases ready for trial. When both parties to the case agree, a magistrate judge may be asked to decide some criminal and civil trials.

Majority Opinion: A written explanation of the decision handed down by a majority of the court (on the Supreme Court if all the justices are participating, five justices constitute a majority). (See also Concurring Opinion; Dissenting Opinion; Plurality Opinion.)

Mandamus: Literally, "we command." A writ that orders a lower court or an official to perform some act. The Supreme Court considers it an extraordinary writ (one that should only be used when all else fails) and rarely issues one.

Master: A person appointed by the Supreme Court to hear the evidence and recommend a decision in a case in which the Court has original jurisdiction. Generally, only one or two original jurisdiction cases come before the Court each term. (See Original Jurisdiction.)

Miranda Rule: See Fifth Amendment.

Mistrial: A trial that has been made invalid because of a fundamental error. When a mistrial is declared, the trial must start again from the very beginning—the selection of a new jury.

Modify: To change or alter. A decision may be modified when an appeals court agrees with only part of the decision the lower court has reached. For example, the Supreme Court may "modify" a decision of the U.S. Court of Appeals for the Second Circuit.

Moot: A **moot issue** is one that is undecided; it has not yet been settled by a court and is still arguable. A **moot case** seeks a judgment to settle an abstract question so it need not be decided at trial.

Motion: An application asking a court to issue an order or to make a ruling in one's favor. It may be either oral or written. For example, a defendant may make a motion that his case be dismissed for lack of evidence.

N.

National Archives and Records Administration (NARA): The place where official records of all three branches of government are stored. After five years the Supreme Court sends material, for example, briefs, along to NARA. Stored material may be used for research purposes in accord with the rules of the Court.

Ninth Amendment (1791): A part of the Bill of Rights, this constitutional amendment has been seldom cited by the Supreme Court. It reads, "The enumeration in the Constitution, of certain rights, shall not be construed to deny or disparage others retained by the people."

It did, however, come into play in the 1965 case, *Griswold v. Connecticut*. Here, by a vote of 7–2, the Court upheld the right of personal privacy, saying that the state could not interfere with a married couple's right to use contraceptives.

Nolo Contendere: Latin for "no contest." For a criminal sentence, it has the same effect as a plea of guilty, but it may not be considered an admission of guilt for any other purpose.

Nominations to the Court: The Constitution says that the president "shall nominate, and by and with the Advice and Consent of the Senate, shall appoint," among others, justices of the Supreme Court. The Senate treats such nominations as it does any other measure: through the committee and subcommittee process.

Since 1868, nominations for Supreme Court justices

have gone to the Senate Committee on the Judiciary. Both the nominee and others appear at hearings to give the committee insight into the nominee's fitness for the Court, background, qualifications, and views on constitutional law. (See Original Intent.)

The committee may report a nomination favorably, unfavorably, or without recommendation, or it may take no action at all. A majority vote of the Senate is needed for final passage. (See also American Bar Association Committee on Federal Judiciary.)

O.

Obiter Dictum: Often referred to simply as **dictum** or **dicta.** It's a statement made by a judge that is incidental to the question before him. It's a kind of "by the way," and it's usually not binding on any future cases.

Opinion: A judge's written explanation of a decision of the court or of a majority of the judges. (See also Concurring Opinion; Dissenting Opinion; Majority Opinion.)

Oral Argument: Legal arguments presented to a court, they are meant to add to the information already supplied in submitted briefs. Oral arguments before the Supreme Court are limited to thirty minutes a side. Sometimes there's a lot of back and forth between an attorney and the justices, and much of the allotted time may be used in answering justices' questions.

The petitioner or appellant, the side bringing the case, is the first to speak. The Supreme Court rules warn that an "oral argument read from a prepared text [is] not favored."

Orders List: A summary in list form of the Supreme Court's business on a particular day. Among other things it lists cases the Court has decided it will and will not review. Although officially designated as the "Order List," it is almost always referred to as the "Orders List." Orders Lists are printed at the back of the *United States Reports*. The volume in which a list appears is printed at the top of the list. Orders Lists may be obtained from the Public Information Office.

An Abbreviated Order List

[*Note: The original ran ten pages.*]

(ORDER LIST: 517 U.S.)

MONDAY, APRIL 22, 1996

CERTIORARI—SUMMARY DISPOSITION

95-642 FRIEND, FRED A. V. UNITED STATES

The petition for rehearing is granted. The order entered January 22, 1996, denying the petition for a writ of certiorari is vacated. The petition for a writ of certiorari is granted, the judgment is vacated and the case is remanded to the United States Court of Appeals for the Eighth Circuit for further consideration in light of *Bailey v. United States*, 516 U.S. __ (1995).

ORDERS IN PENDING CASES

A-796 MICHAEL ELIAS V. UNITED STATES

The application for stay addressed to Justice Stevens and referred to the Court is denied.

A-835 JAKE AYERS, ET AL. V. KIRK FORDICE, GOVERNOR OF MISSISSIPPI, ET AL.

The application for stay of an order of the United States District Court for the Northern District of Mississippi presented to Justice

Petitioner: The person who asks a court to begin a proceeding, or the person appealing a judgment. (See Respondent.)

Petit Jury: Usually made up of six to twelve people (a grand jury is usually made up of twenty-three), it's the ordinary trial jury whose job it is to decide civil and criminal cases.

Plaintiff: The person who files the complaint in a civil lawsuit.

Plea Bargaining: The accused admits to the crime, and the prosecutor promises that a lighter sentence will be imposed. Sometimes the accused admits to a lesser offense, for example, manslaughter instead of murder. The accused gives up certain constitutional rights, such as trial by jury, in the process. In 1970, in *Brady v. United States*, the Supreme Court recognized the practice and gave the okay for its use. (See also Settlement.)

Plurality Opinion: Here, the court's decision has been agreed to by a majority, but the reasoning behind that decision has been agreed to by less than a majority. In other words there are more justices issuing concurring opinions than there are justices signing on to the original opinion. (See Concurring Opinion; Majority Opinion.)

Precedent: A court decision in an earlier case with facts and law similar to those in a dispute currently before a court. Precedent will ordinarily govern the decision of a later case, unless a party can show that the case was wrongly decided or that it differed in some significant way from the current case. (See also Common Law; Stare Decisis.)

Pretrial Conference: A meeting of the judge and lawyers to discuss which matters should be presented to the jury, to review evidence and witnesses, to set a timetable, and to discuss a possible settlement of the case.

Prima Facie: Latin for "at first view," "on its face." A prima facie case is one that doesn't require further support; the evidence in your favor is so strong that the other party *must* mount a defense.

Privileges and Immunities: See Fourteenth Amendment.

Probation: A sentencing alternative to imprisonment in which the court releases a convicted defendant under supervision as long as certain conditions are observed, for example, weekly visits to a probation officer.

Procedure: The rules for the conduct of a lawsuit; there are rules of civil, criminal, evidence, bankruptcy, and appellate procedure.

Pro Se: Literally, "on one's own behalf." In courts, it refers to persons who present their own cases without benefit of lawyers.

Prosecute: To charge someone with a crime.

Prosecutor: Someone who tries a criminal case on behalf of the government. U.S. attorneys are the prosecutors in district courts, and the U.S. solicitor general handles the job for the government in cases before the Supreme Court.

2.

Quash: To annul or make void by judicial decision. Subpoenas, orders, injunctions, etc. can all be quashed.

Quorum: The number of people who must be present in order that business can be conducted. In the Supreme Court six justices constitute a quorum.

R.

Ratio Decidendi: The principle that determined the outcome of a case; it becomes the ground upon which decisions in future cases will rest.

Record: A written account of all the acts and proceedings in a lawsuit.

Recusal: Abstention. If a judge has a personal interest in a case, he removes himself from the proceedings. Recusal is a way of protecting those involved from any preexisting bias the judge may have.

Remand: When a higher court sends a case back to the lower court for further proceedings. (See also Affirm; Reverse.)

Reserve Powers Clause: See Tenth Amendment.

Respondent: The party who must answer the claims of an appellant or petitioner.

Reverse: When a higher court disagrees with the decision reached by a lower court, it overturns that lower court's decision. When the Supreme Court reverses a decision, the case is usually sent back (remanded) to the lower court for a new trial, one that takes into account the reasoning behind the Supreme Court's opinion. (See also Affirm; Remand.)

There is no court higher than the Supreme Court, so there are only three ways in which a Supreme Court's decision can be changed:

1. Congress may pass a law affecting the decision. They did this when they passed the Civil Rights Act of 1991, overturning the Supreme Court's 1989 decision in *Ward's Cove Packing Co. v. Atonio*. The decision had said that even if an employee proved the company was discriminating against him, it was okay for an employer to fire or demote him if it was necessary to the business. The 1991 act made it illegal to intentionally discriminate by claiming "business necessity."

2. An amendment may be added to the Constitution that changes the Court's ruling. See the Eleventh Amendment, which overturned *Chisholm v. Georgia*.

3. The Court may decide a case down the road in a way that negates its original opinion. *Brown v. Board of Education* was such a case. See the Fourteenth Amendment.

Riding Circuit: At one time Supreme Court justices traveled twice a year to the appeals courts in a given circuit (jurisdiction) to hear cases and hand out justice. The roads were bad, the inns inhospitable, the workload heavy, and the distance from family great. In 1891, Congress passed the Circuit Court Act, establishing circuit courts with their own judges. Today, a Supreme Court justice is assigned to each of the thirteen judicial circuits to hear emergency stay applications, for example, in capital cases, but he doesn't actually sit on the circuit court.

Robes: In the early days, Supreme Court justices wore scarlet-faced robes trimmed with gold piping (some justices even wore wigs). Sometime around 1801, the ornate robes were replaced with plain black ones, and the wearing of wigs was discontinued.

Robing Room: The small room where the Supreme Court justices store their robes and put them on before entering the courtroom. It's located next to the conference room on the main floor of the Supreme Court Building.

Rulemaking Power of the Supreme Court: Congress has from time to time given the Supreme Court the power to set out rules of procedure to be followed by the lower courts of the United States. The statutes that are currently in force have rules ordered by the Court that govern civil and criminal cases, appellate proceedings, and the trial of misdemeanors before U.S. magistrate judges.

Rule of Four: It's an unwritten rule that a case will not be heard by the Supreme Court unless at least four justices vote to review it.

Rules of the Supreme Court: From time to time the Court issues a set of rules that concern the workings of the Court as well as the procedures attorneys must follow when bringing a case before it. Rules may be suggested by the justices themselves, a member of the Bar, or by a committee created by the Court to do just that. Rule changes are agreed to by consensus rather than by a formal vote. (See Appendix C for a complete set of the most recent Rules; and Chapter 5, "Reaching Out," for the Internet site.)

S.

Seal: The Supreme Court seal is in the custody of the clerk of the Court. It's stamped on official papers, such as the certificates attorneys receive when they are admitted to practice before the Bar of the Supreme Court. The seal is similar to the Great Seal of the United States, but it has only one star beneath the eagle's claw—thus symbolizing that the Constitution mandates but one Supreme Court.

Search and Seizure: See Fourth Amendment.

Second Amendment (1791): Part of the Bill of Rights, it says, "A well regulated Militia, being necessary to the security of a free State, the right of the people to keep and bear Arms, shall not be infringed." If a federal gun-control law doesn't interfere with a state militia, the Supreme Court has said that the amendment doesn't apply; the right to bear arms is not considered to have been infringed.

Self-Incrimination: See Fifth Amendment.

Senate Judiciary Committee: See Nominations to the Court.

Seniority: It refers to the length of time a justice (excluding the chief justice, who always is considered most senior) has served on the Supreme Court. Seniority determines such things as the order in which justices speak and vote at conference, where justices sit in the courtroom, and their choice of chambers. The justice who has been on the Court longest has the most seniority—he's the senior associate justice. The newest justice—the most junior justice—takes on the job of doorkeeper and messenger during the Court's conferences.

Sentence: The punishment ordered by a court for a defendant convicted of a crime.

Separate but Equal: See Fourteenth Amendment.

Sequester: "To separate." Sometimes juries are housed and fed at the court's expense so that they may not fall prey to outside influences. A jury may be sequestered for the whole trial or only when deliberating the case.

Seriatim: From the Latin, meaning "one by one"; "individually." Separate opinions were at one time written by each Supreme Court justice, but this practice was abandoned in the early 1800s.

Service of Process: The delivery of writs or summonses or other court papers to the appropriate party.

Session: The time when the Supreme Court is at work. The Court's schedule calls for it to be in session for approximately two weeks and then to be in recess for two weeks.

A **special session** may be held to deal with urgent matters that cannot be postponed until the next session. For example, the Court held a special session in 1953 to hear the case of *Rosenberg v. United States*. Julius and Ethel Rosenberg had been convicted of spying for the Soviet Union, and Justice Douglas had ordered a stay of execution. The Court voted to lift the stay and the Rosenbergs were executed.

Settlement: Parties to a lawsuit may resolve their differences—reach a settlement—without going to trial. Settlements often involve the payment of compensation by one party to satisfy the claims of the other. (See also Plea Bargaining.)

Seventh Amendment (1791): Part of the Bill of Rights, it guarantees your right to a jury trial in a civil case before a federal court, if the amount you're fighting over is more than $20.

Sidebar: A conference between judge and lawyers held out of earshot of the jury and spectators.

Sixth Amendment (1791): It guarantees your right to a fair trial. This amendment, which is part of the Bill of Rights, entitles you to a speedy trial by an impartial jury;

to be informed of the charges against you; and to confront your accusers. It allows you to compel witnesses to testify in your defense and assures you of competent counsel.

In a 1938 case, *Johnson v. Zerbst*, the Court in a 6–2 decision (Justice Cardozo didn't participate), focused on the right ". . . to have the Assistance of Counsel for [your] defence." The Court found that federal courts can't deprive a person of life or liberty without his having the aid of an attorney, unless the defendant waives that right.

In 1975, in *Taylor v. Louisiana*, the Court focused on a state exempting women from jury duty. In an 8–1 decision it held that Louisiana, by excluding women, had been violating that part of the amendment that guarantees that to be fair a jury must be chosen from the community in which the crime was committed. The Court's decision overruled its earlier one in *Hoyt v. Florida* (1961), upholding a woman's exemption because her place was in the home.

Slip Opinion: The unedited but complete version of a Court's decision. It's printed in booklet form and made available within three days of the decision's having been reached. A notice at the top of the opinion asks readers to notify the reporter of decisions of any "typographical or other formal errors, in order that corrections may be made before the preliminary print goes to press."

Slip opinions are printed by a private company under contract with the Government Printing Office. (The GPO supplies copies to the Judiciary Committees of both the House and Senate, and the Department of Justice.) The Court orders four hundred copies of each opinion to be distributed by the Public Information Office on an as-requested basis. Quantities are also ordered by the Administrative Office of the U.S. Courts and distributed to federal judges.

Solicitor General: Appointed by the president, the solicitor general or a member of his staff represents the U.S.

government in cases before the Supreme Court. (See Chapter 1, "The Stage and the Players." See also U.S. Attorney.)

Standing to Sue: To possess the legal right to go to court to challenge another, including the government.

Stare Decisis: Literally, "let the decision stand"; the doctrine to uphold precedents. It means that in similar cases, past judicial decisions should be accepted as the authorities. (See Precedent.)

Statute: A written law passed by a legislature. A law enacted by the U.S. Congress is a **federal statute;** one enacted by a state legislature is a **state statute.** A statute violating the Constitution may, if challenged, be struck down by the Supreme Court. In 1849, in what came to be known as the *Passenger cases* (*Smith v. Turner* and *Norris v. Boston*) the Court, citing the Constitution's commerce power, struck down state laws that put a tax on passengers entering U.S. ports.

Statute of Limitations: A law that sets the time within which parties must take action to enforce their rights. It's designed to prevent stale claims where memories may fade.

Stay: An order that stops or suspends any action until some particular event occurs or the stay is lifted by the court. A justice of the Supreme Court, acting alone, may issue a stay to stop a lower court's acting on a particular matter.

Subpoena: Its official name is Subpoena ad Testificandum. It's a court order that commands a witness to appear and give testimony. If you disobey it, you may be found in contempt of court and duly punished.

Subpoena Duces Tecum: A court order that's issued at the request of one party to a case, asking a witness to produce any relevant documents under his control, for example, business or tax records.

Summary Judgment: A decision arrived at by a judge without a trial; it's made on the basis of statements and evidence presented for the record. It's used when there is no dispute as to the facts of the case and one party is entitled to judgment as a matter of law.

Supreme Court Bar: (1) Attorneys who can practice before the Supreme Court. (For the requirements to be admitted to the Supreme Court Bar, see Appendix C, Rule 5.) If an attorney has been disbarred or suspended from practice in any other court, or has conducted himself in any way unbecoming to a member of the Bar, he's suspended from practice before the Court and has forty days in which to respond to the charge. (2) The bronze railing in the courtroom of the Supreme Court that separates the public seating from the courtroom proper.

Supreme Court Historical Society: A private, nonprofit group whose aim is to increase the public's knowledge of the Supreme Court. It supports historical research and collects Court memorabilia. It manages the gift shop on the ground floor of the Supreme Court Building; the place where you can buy books and other Court-related material.

Supreme Court Reporter: Published by West Publishing Company, it's one of the unofficial records of Supreme Court decisions. The decisions are the same as in the *United States Reports*—the Supreme Court's official record. Among other material, West gives summaries of all cases, and tables of key words and phrases. In case citations it's designated "S. Ct." (See Citation; and Chapter 6.)

Syllabus: The headnote, or summary, that appears at the beginning of each printed Supreme Court case. It's prepared by the reporter of decisions and helps a reader get a quick fix on what the case is all about. Syllabi include such things as a case's background, the justices' legal reasoning in reaching their opinions, and of course, whether the lower court's ruling has been affirmed or denied. It concludes with the lineup, which reveals how each justice voted.

The following statement appears at the beginning of each syllabus: "NOTE: Where it is feasible, a syllabus (headnote) will be released, as is being done in connection with this case, at the time the opinion is issued. The syllabus constitutes no part of the opinion of the Court but has been prepared by the Reporter of Decisions for the convenience of the reader."

"Taking the Fifth": A way of saying someone is exercising his right against self-incrimination. The right is guaranteed by the Fifth Amendment, which explains the phrase. (See Fifth Amendment.)

Temporary Restraining Order: It prohibits a person from an action that is likely to cause irreparable harm. It differs from an injunction in that it may be granted immediately, without notice to the opposing party, and without a hearing. It is intended to last only until a hearing can be held.

Tenth Amendment (1791): Known as the Reserved Powers Amendment, it states, "The powers not delegated to the United States by the Constitution, nor prohibited by it to the States, are reserved to the States respectively, or to the people." It was included in the Bill of Rights to keep the federal government from wielding powers it was not specifically given in the Constitution, for example, the establishment of local and state police forces.

Term of the Supreme Court: The Supreme Court has one term each year—it begins on the first Monday in October and lasts until the Court's business is completed, usually in late June or early July. A term is designated by the year in which it began. For example, the term beginning in October 1997 and officially ending in October 1998 is called the 1997 term. (See also Session.)

Test Case: A lawsuit whose purpose is to see if a law or legal principle will stand up in court. A group may intentionally break the law in order to test that law's constitutionality. For example, when Congress passed the Flag Protection Act of 1989, which forbade burning the American flag, a flag was purposely burned and the case ended up in the Supreme Court. In *United States v. Eichman* the Court held the Act unconstitutional as applied and dismissed the charges.

Often when there is a group of similar suits pending, the one that is most representative or thought most likely to succeed will become the test case. The outcome will be pertinent to the other cases when they are tried.

Testimony: Evidence presented by a witness during a trial or before a grand jury.

Tort: A civil wrong or breach of a duty to another person as outlined by law. A very common tort is negligent operation of a motor vehicle that results in property damage and/or personal injury.

Transcript: A written, word-for-word record of what was said. It's made as the proceeding occurs, whether in a trial or during some other conversation, for example, a hearing or an oral deposition.

Trial Docket: A court calendar listing the cases to be tried. It's prepared by the clerk of the court.

$\mathscr{U}$.

United States Attorney: A lawyer, appointed by the president, in each judicial district to prosecute and defend cases for the federal government. The solicitor general fills this role in cases before the Supreme Court.

United States Court of Appeals for the Federal Circuit: This appellate court's jurisdiction is nationwide, and it hears cases appealed from a few specialized lower courts, for example, the U.S. Court of International Trade, the U.S. Court of Federal Claims, and the U.S. Court of Veterans Appeals. Cases lost here may be appealed directly to the Supreme Court. For more on this court, see Appendix A.

United States Court of Federal Claims: This court's nationwide jurisdiction is over claims seeking money judgments against the United States. Judgments may be appealed to the United States Court of Appeals for the Federal Circuit and from there on to the Supreme Court. For more on this court, see Appendix A.

United States Court of International Trade: It has jurisdiction over any civil action against the United States arising from federal laws governing import transactions. Here cases may be tried before a jury, and appeals go to the U.S. Court of Appeals for the Federal Circuit and then, if appropriate, to the Supreme Court. For more on this court, see Appendix A.

United States Court of Military Appeals: Appeals from court-martial convictions for all military services come to this court. If lost here, some cases may go on to the Supreme Court. For more on this court, see Appendix A.

United States Court of Veterans Appeals: It is the only place to go to have decisions of the Board of Veterans Appeals reviewed. From here, decisions are appealed to the United States Court of Appeals for the Federal Circuit and then to the Supreme Court. For more on this court, see Appendix A.

United States Courts of Appeals: Intermediate appellate courts that may review all final decisions and certain interlocutory decisions of district courts. They also have the power to review and enforce orders of many federal administrative bodies. The decisions of the courts of appeals are final, but they may be appealed to the Supreme Court. There are twelve courts of appeals that serve the fifty states and the District of Columbia, and a thirteenth for the Federal Circuit. For more on these courts, see Appendix A.

United States District Courts: District courts are the trial courts of the federal system—the places where both criminal and civil cases are initially filed and tried. Each state has at least one district court and some of the larger states have as many as four. Cases lost in a district court can be appealed, as a right, to the appropriate court of appeals. For example, if you lost your case in the District Court of the Eastern District of New York, you could appeal to the U.S. Court of Appeals for the Second Circuit. If the Second Circuit turned you down, you could try the Supreme Court. For more on the U.S. district courts, see Appendix A.

United States Law Week: An unofficial record of Supreme Court decisions published by the Bureau of National Affairs. In case citations it appears as "U.S.L.W." (See Citation; and Chapter 6.)

3

The Route to the Supreme Court

Who Gets to Be Heard

The Supreme Court cannot initiate cases, and not all cases are eligible for Supreme Court review.

Who Gets to Be Heard by the Supreme Court

The Supreme Court has two types of jurisdiction—the legal authority to decide and hear cases—original jurisdiction and appellate jurisdiction.

ORIGINAL JURISDICTION

The Supreme Court has original jurisdiction over several small but important categories of cases. That means if a case falls into one of these categories the parties can bring their dispute *directly* to the Supreme Court. The power of original jurisdiction is set out in Article III, section 2, of the Constitution.

The Court has original *and* exclusive jurisdiction in all controversies between two or more states. In such disputes only the Supreme Court has the power to hear the case. Typically, disputes between states that come to the Court involve conflicting property claims. For example, *Louisiana v. Mississippi* (decided October 31, 1995) concerned the states' boundaries along a seven-mile stretch of the Mississippi River. (Louisiana lost, tried for a rehearing, and lost again.)

The Supreme Court has original *but not* exclusive jurisdiction in cases involving ambassadors, other public ministers, and consuls; all controversies between the United States and a state; and all actions or proceedings by a state against the citizens of another state or against aliens.

Of all the cases brought to the Supreme Court, only one or two are original jurisdiction cases. When one does reach the Court, it's the Court's practice to appoint a "Master" to hear the evidence, determine facts, and recommend a decision. The Court reviews the Master's findings and recommendations in the light of legal arguments made by the opposing parties and reaches its decision.

APPELLATE JURISDICTION

The Supreme Court has appellate jurisdiction—the authority to hear cases brought on appeal from lower federal courts and from state courts when an issue concerning federal law or the U.S. Constitution is involved.

Appellate jurisdiction has been given to the Supreme Court by various statutes enacted by Congress, and Congress can change the Court's appellate jurisdiction by enacting new statutes. It cannot, however, change the original jurisdiction of the Court.

The Way to the Supreme Court

In order to come before the Supreme Court, a case that falls under the Court's appellate jurisdiction takes one of two roads: it travels up through the federal court system or up through the state court system.

THE FEDERAL COURT ROUTE

Cases may be brought by individuals, or companies, or state or local government agencies. No matter by whom they're brought, all travel the same route.

1. Case is tried in a U.S. district court: The district courts are the trial courts of general federal jurisdiction. The cases they hear may be between citizens of different states or between the United States and foreign citizens. They may also hear criminal cases involving fraud, tax evasion, and counterfeiting, as well as cases based on federal laws and orders. The cases may be either civil or criminal in nature.

A typical *civil* case would proceed this way: complaint filed, answer filed, discovery proceedings, motions filed relating to discovery matters, other pretrial proceedings, trial by a judge or a jury, verdict.

In criminal cases, the government is the plaintiff. A typical *criminal* action would go like this: defendant arrested and a complaint filed, preliminary hearing, grand jury returns an indictment, discovery proceedings, motions filed, trial, opening statements, government prosecutor's case, presentation of evidence, defendant's case, government's rebuttal case, closing arguments, judge's instruction to the jury, deliberation, verdict.

2. Loser takes his case to the appropriate U.S. Court of Appeals: Appeals are based on the loser's contention that the lower court made an error or was somehow unjust in coming to its decision.

The courts of appeals are intermediate appellate courts created by an act of March 3, 1891, to relieve the Supreme Court of considering all appeals in cases originally decided by the federal trial courts. Cases from the district courts are reviewable on appeal by the applicable court of appeals. For example, a case heard in the Northern District of Ohio will be appealed to the Court of Appeals of the Sixth Circuit. (For a closer look at the federal court system, see Appendix A.) These courts are empowered to review all final decisions and certain interlocutory (temporary) decisions of the district courts. They also are empowered to review and enforce orders of many federal administrative bodies. The decisions of the courts of appeals are final, but if the loser chooses to pursue the matter, they are subject to discretionary review or appeal in the Supreme Court.

3. Loser takes his case to the Supreme Court.

THE STATE COURT ROUTE

The states each have their own court systems. Many states have two different sets of trial courts: one to handle minor cases (these may be local courts such as justice's courts, police courts, and municipal courts) and another to handle major cases. These courts, too, have different names in different states. They may be referred to as circuit courts, district courts, courts of common pleas, and oddly, as in New York State, the supreme court.

1. Case brought in state trial court: At this point, as in the federal court system, if the loser feels there has been an error or injustice committed by the trial court he may appeal the decision.

2. Loser takes his case to an intermediate state appeals court: Not all the states have intermediate appellate courts so some cases will go directly to the highest state court.

3. Loser takes his case to the highest state court: In same states it's called the state supreme court, in others the court of appeals, the supreme judicial court, or the supreme court of appeals. Whatever its name, it's the highest state court and its decisions can be appealed directly to the U.S. Supreme Court. Unlike other appeals, however, certain special conditions must be met—the case must either have denied the validity of a treaty or statute of the United States, or a constitutional question must be involved.

4. Loser takes his case to the Supreme Court.

4

From Introduction to Decision

The Road Taken by a Petition for a Writ of Certiorari

THE SUPREME COURT PACING THE FLOOR TRYING TO REACH A TOUGH DECISION

After a trip through either the federal or the state court systems, a case comes to the Supreme Court via one of four roads: through a petition for an extraordinary writ, a request for certification, on appeal, or by a petition for a writ of certiorari.

A petition for an extraordinary writ: This is the road least taken. You don't have a right to the various kinds of extraordinary writs—all are issued at the Court's discretion. Among other things, the petition for an extraordinary writ must show that exceptional circumstances warrant the exercise of the Court's discretionary powers, and that you cannot get adequate relief in any other form or from any other court. A petition for a writ of habeas corpus is an example of this little-used device.

A request for certification: Sometimes a lower court, most often a court of appeals, needs some help. A question of law has come up in a case before the lower court, and it feels it needs the insight of the Supreme Court to decide the issue.

The certificate it submits to the Supreme Court contains a statement of the nature of the case and the facts on which the questions of law arise. The Court ponders the problem. It may give the lower court an instruction, and such instructions must be followed, or it may decide that the case record should be brought before the justices for argument at the highest level. (A case record includes all the items introduced into evidence as well as the papers, for example, briefs and motions filed in the lower court.)

An appeal: Almost all cases brought on appeal do come before the Supreme Court for discussion. The person seeking review by the Court must explain why his case qualifies (meets the Court's jurisdictional requirements) and why it should be heard.

Most cases that reach the Supreme Court by this route are decided summarily; no oral arguments are heard and no formal opinions are given. The justices decide the case in conference. The released decision is labeled per curiam (by the Court), and not signed by any justice.

A petition for a writ of certiorari (cert.): Most cases that reach the Supreme Court come down this road. Asking for "cert." is the way losers in a lower court ask the Supreme Court to review their cases. A petition for cert. presents the disputed question of law for review and states the statutory provisions believed to confer jurisdiction on the Supreme Court. It is up to the Court to determine whether it will grant certiorari and hear a case. No law says it must.

If cert. is denied you still may try to have the Court listen to your case. You may, within twenty-five days of the Court's decision, petition for a rehearing. Grounds for a rehearing are "limited to intervening circumstances of a substantial or controlling effect or to other substantial grounds not previously presented," so states the Court's Rule 44 (2).

Most of the hundreds of petitions for writs of certiorari are denied, but a few do go on to be heard by the full Court. For example, the Eighth Amendment case of *Solem v. Helm* began in the United States District Court for the District of South Dakota; was appealed to the U.S. Court of Appeals for the Eighth Circuit, which reversed the district court's decision; and, on certiorari, was affirmed by the Supreme Court.

One Case's Journey

1. A petition for a writ of certiorari is sent to the clerk of the Court, where it is examined to make sure that it's in the proper form.

2. Once given the clerk's okay, the necessary fee of $300 is paid and the petition is numbered and placed on a docket. (The U.S. government and people who are indigent and filing in the manner of a pauper *[in forma pauperis]* are excused from paying this fee.)

A petition number consists of the year and a consecutive case number. For example, the third case filed in the 1997 term would be 97-3, the thirty-third 97-33. In forma pauperis cases contain the year and begin with the number 5001; for example, the third case filed in 1997 would be 97-5003, the thirty-third 97-5033.

3. It is the justices' duty to look at all the cases on the docket. But because a flood of petitions are received weekly, different justices have come up with different ways to keep from being swamped: some read through the cert. petitions themselves; some lighten the task by reading only summaries that their clerks, who do the actual reading, prepare. A cert. pool has also been used. That's where the clerks of several of the justices work together; they read the cases and then write a pool memorandum. These memos are passed along to the participating justices.

4. Created by the chief justice, a discuss list—a list of the cases he thinks should be looked at by the Court—is sent around to the associate justices. (Most cases brought on appeal make the list, but few brought on cert. ever do.) The Court will discuss these cases in conference and vote on which ones will get a full hearing.

Any justice may ask that a particular case be included on the discuss list and it will be added. If a case doesn't make the discuss list, it will never be reviewed by the Court.

5. At conference the justices decide whether to grant or deny review. The business of a conference is strictly between the justices; no outsiders, including law clerks, are present and no minutes are taken.

The chief justice briefly outlines the case and the justices (in order of seniority) give their views, usually indicating how they intend to vote. If there doesn't seem to be a consensus either for or against taking on the case, a formal vote is taken. Even if all nine justices are present, the unwritten "rule of four" says that it takes four yes votes in order for a case to be scheduled to be heard.

A justice who feels strongly about a case that's been turned down for review may ask that it be reconsidered at the next conference. In the interim he may lobby the other justices, hoping to gain the necessary four votes in the next conference.

The justices may decide to review a case but hear no oral arguments. Instead, they'll make their decision on the basis of written material alone. Decisions in such cases are made per curiam ("by the court")—all the justices agree and no signed opinion is handed down.

On the other hand, the Court may decide that the case merits the full treatment—oral argument and a decision complete with concurring and dissenting opinions.

6. The results of the conference, whether petitions have or have not been approved for review, are listed on a certified orders list and the list is released to the public.

Although the Court rarely explains its reasons for denying a case review, a justice who has been lobbying for one but has failed to get the necessary four votes may note his dissent from the Court's decision, and his reasons for it.

7. Oral arguments are scheduled by the clerk of the Court. Most often cases come before the Court in the same order in which they were reviewed. The Supreme Court's Rule 27 says that "A case ordinarily will not be called for argument less than two weeks after the brief on the merits for the respondent or appellee is due." The clerk lets counsel know when they are due to appear for oral arguments.

8. Counsel for both sides submit their briefs. The rules say that briefs "shall be concise, logically arranged with proper headings, and free of irrelevant, immaterial, or scandalous matter." They must also follow rules that lay down everything from the number of pages to the color of their covers. For example, the cover of a petitioner's brief on the merits of a case must be light blue.

A petitioner must file forty copies of his brief within forty-five days of receiving the order granting a writ of certiorari. The respondent files his forty copies within thirty days after receiving his opponent's brief. Thirty days after receiving this brief the petitioner may file forty copies of his reply brief. The clerk of the Court is the person to be asked for time extensions.

9. The justices review the briefs and records that they have received from counsel. With the help of their clerks they may check citations and research material. At times justices prepare the questions they'll ask in advance of the oral arguments.

10. Oral arguments are heard. The Rules of the Supreme Court ask attorneys to assume that the justices have read their briefs, and remind the lawyers that their oral arguments should be used to emphasize and clarify these written arguments, not restate them. In reality, justices may not have read every brief, so anyone making an oral argument tries to make it as complete as possible. The Rules go on to say that reading from a prepared text "will be frowned upon." Before oral arguments get under way, lawyers meet with the clerk of the Court for a briefing explaining courtroom procedure.

It is the petitioner who starts the ball rolling, and he may if he chooses conclude the argument as well. He presents his complete case and doesn't reserve any meaningful points for rebuttal. Unless the Court says otherwise, each side is allowed thirty minutes for its argument. They don't have to use up all their time but, on the other hand, additional time is rarely granted.

Justices can and do interrupt during the session, either to ask questions or simply to make remarks. They may interrupt as often as they like, and the time they use is deducted from a side's allotted thirty minutes. When a lawyer's time is up, it's up, and he'll find himself allowed to complete his sentence but unable to add another word.

Only one attorney is heard for each side. A counsel who has filed an amicus ("a friend of the court") brief may argue orally on the side of the party he favors, but only with its consent, and the time he uses will be subtracted from that party's thirty minutes.

At the conclusion of oral arguments the chief justice announces that "The case is submitted."

Oral arguments are taped and transcribed both by the Court and by a private company the Court contracts with to do this job. The transcripts are complete unless the chief justice or presiding justice asks that something be omitted. When a justice has asked a question, the letter Q is substituted for his name.

The tapes are kept by the marshal during the term the argument is presented. Except in rare cases, they can be heard only by the justices and their clerks. When the term is over, the tapes are sent to the National Archives and Records Administration (NARA). NARA sells copies of the transcripts and allows people to listen to them after applying for permission to do so. However, even before the term is concluded, transcripts may be bought from the private firm that produces them.

11. The justices meet to decide the cases whose oral arguments they've heard. These conferences are again held in strictest secrecy, with none but the justices present.

The chief justice runs the show and is the first to speak on each case. The justices follow him, speaking in order of seniority. A vote is taken and the majority wins, which means that if all nine justices are present five votes are needed to reach a decision. At least six justices (a quorum) must be participating for a vote to be taken. In the case of a tie vote, the lower court's decision is left standing. Because down the line (see step 15) the Court may change its decision, neither the outcome of the votes taken in conference nor how each justice voted is released to the public.

12. At the conference, once the case has been decided, either the chief justice or the senior associate justice, whoever voted with the majority, is the person who decides which justice will draft the majority opinion.

When choosing who will write the opinion the justice assigning the case may consider which justice is interested in the topic or has a special expertise in it, a justice's current workload, or even how committed he is to the issue at hand; an extreme view may not be wanted. The assignment may be made as either a punishment or as a reward. In an important case the assigning justice may wish to assign himself the job. He may even change his vote to put himself in the majority in order to do so.

13. The justices now focus on the written opinion. The necessary research is begun by their clerks, citations are found, and legal arguments constructed.

The justice assigned to write the majority opinion begins work on a draft, one that he hopes will reflect the Court's consensus.

Justices who agree with his opinion may send along memos with suggestions for citations, precedents, and legal reasoning.

During this time, a justice who agrees with the majority but who has reached his conclusion running along different tracks, may decide to write his own concurring opinion.

And, of course, any justice who is adamantly opposed to the majority's view may be hard at work on a dissenting opinion, which he too hopes will attract other justices. (A justice may dissent without writing an opinion; he is simply recorded as dissenting.)

14. Drafts of the majority, concurring, and dissenting opinions are circulated among the justices.

15. Although some cases will be concluded quickly, others will require much discussion and reworking of the circulated draft opinions. Memos will fly from chamber to chamber and negotiations will begin. The justice writing the majority opinion may find it necessary to alter some of his words in order to be assured of maintaining his majority. At times, the author of a minority opinion will attract other justices to his cause, and what started out as a minority dissent can end up as a majority opinion. Sometimes complete agreement is hard to come by. For example, in the 1971 Pentagon Papers case dealing with freedom of the press, each of the nine justices wrote a separate opinion. Although unsigned (per curiam) each justice expressed his own views of the 6–3 decision.

16. When the dust settles, the Supreme Court may decide to affirm (to approve) the lower court's decision, or to remand (send the case back for further deliberation) its decision; or it may reverse the lower court's decision. When it does the latter, it generally sends the case back for a new trial, one taking into account the reasoning behind the Supreme Court's decision.

17. The reporter of decisions adds a syllabus (a headnote) summarizing the decision at the beginning of the opinion. At the end of the syllabus is the "lineup," which shows how each justice voted. The final versions of the majority, concurring, and dissenting opinions are sent to the Government Printing Office, which prints slip opinions for distribution to the lower courts. The GPO also prints the opinion that will appear in *U.S. Reports*, the official record of Supreme Court decisions.

18. Opinions are announced on Tuesdays and Wednesdays during the weeks the Court is hearing oral argu-

and, if you choose the right day, hear oral arguments; you can have a say in how the Senate views a candidate for Supreme Court justice; and you can keep abreast of the Court's decisions via the Internet.

Visiting the Court

The Supreme Court Building is located at 1 First Street, S.E., Washington, D.C. It's open year-round, Monday to Friday from 9:00 A.M. to 4:30 P.M.; it's closed on legal holidays. When the Court is not in session, you can attend a free lecture on its history. Lectures are given in the courtroom by the staff of the curator's office every hour on the half hour beginning at 9:30 A.M. and concluding at 3:30 P.M.

THE COURT'S SCHEDULE

Each new term begins on the first Monday in October and continues until all the Court's work is concluded.

The Court holds seven two-week sessions, each followed by a two-week recess with longer breaks in December and February. During recesses the justices consider the cases they've heard, take care of Court business, and prepare for the next argument session.

The summer recess usually begins in late June. Special sessions may be called during the summer, but this is rarely done.

There is no set period between when a case is argued and when the Court must hand down its decision. One thing is certain, all cases that have been argued during a term will be decided before the summer recess begins.

Monday: During weeks when the Court is in session, the Court sits from 10:00 A.M. to noon and from

1:00 P.M. to 3:00 P.M. Court business is taken care of first, including the admission of new members to the Supreme Court Bar, and then oral arguments are heard. Typically, two cases are heard in the morning and two in the afternoon. All are open to the public. The oral argument portion of the term ends in late April or early May.

During weeks when oral arguments are not being heard, Monday is the day the Court releases its opinions and the Orders List. A decision is announced by the justice who wrote the majority opinion. Although he may if he wishes read the entire opinion, it is more usual for him to summarize the Court's reasoning in the case. The same holds true for justices who have written dissenting opinions. At this time the Court meets at 10:00 A.M. for sessions that typically last ten to thirty minutes. These sessions are open to the public.

Tuesday: During weeks when the Court is in session it releases its opinions and Orders List and then hears oral arguments. The same hours as on Monday are kept, and the public is welcome.

Wednesday: During weeks when the Court is in session, the Court releases its opinions and hears oral arguments in the morning (open to the public) and holds a conference in the afternoon (closed to the public).

Thursday: No public sessions are held. The justices go about the Court's business, for example, researching cases, writing opinions, and meeting their courts of appeals' obligations.

Friday: During weeks when the Court is in session, conferences are held; they're also held on the last Friday of a recess. Conferences are private, and neither staff nor the public may attend.

IF YOU DO DECIDE TO VISIT

You can call the Public Information Office at (202) 479-3211 to find out if the Court is in session, but even if you can't see it in action, it's still an interesting and awesome place and worth a visit. You don't need to have a ticket to visit the Court, all you have to do is get in line and wait your turn. When Court's in session, two lines form on the plaza in front of the building: one is for people who wish to attend an entire argument, and the other (the three-minute line) is for those who wish to observe the Court only briefly.

There is a security check as you enter the building and again as you enter the courtroom. When Court is in session, you may not bring in cameras, radios, pagers, tape players or recorders, other electronic equipment, hats, overcoats, magazines, books, or briefcases and luggage. You can leave your items in the first-floor checkroom. One last thing: sunglasses may not be worn in the courtroom.

Becoming Part of the Nominating Process

A president takes many factors into consideration before nominating someone to the Supreme Court: the person's ability and reputation; what part of the country he comes from; his politics, ideology, religion; and, most importantly, whether that person will be able to win Senate confirmation. That's where you and I come in.

If you learn a person has been nominated to the Court and have information you think the Senate should hear, you can try to get that word out. One way is to contact a member of the Senate Committee on the Judiciary and ask to be put on the witness list.

To find out who is on the Senate Committee on the

Judiciary look in a copy of the *Congressional Directory*. It is edited by the Joint Committee on Printing and is available from the Government Printing Office. Your local library should have a copy or another book with the same information. Go to the reference section and look for books filed under Dewey decimal number 328.

If you don't have a senator's address, you can write to him care of the U.S. Senate, Washington, D.C. 20510, or you can write to the Judiciary Committee, United States Senate, Washington, D.C. 20510.

You can also contact most senators through their E-mail address. You can find out E-mail addresses by accessing the Senate's home page: **http://www.senate.gov** or try **gopher://ftp.senate.gov** Just click on the home page line: <u>Senators with Constituent E-Mail Addresses</u>.

If you call the committee and ask to be put on the witness list, be sure to send a follow-up letter confirming your request.

There are two other ways you can try to be put on the list to testify: through an advocacy group or through a member's legislative assistant (LA). It may take a long time to sell the LA on the importance of your testifying; remember, he in turn has to sell the idea to the committee staff.

If you're asked to appear either alone or as part of a panel, submit a detailed summary of your testimony. Committee members like to review what you have to say before you say it. Keep your statement short and to the point. Begin by stating your name and address. (If you're speaking for an organization, give its name and address instead of your own.) State your position clearly. Conclude your statement by thanking the committee for giving you the opportunity to express your views and by giving a summary of your basic position.

Surfing the Internet

Unlike the president, vice president, senators, and representatives, Supreme Court justices don't have E-mail addresses; at least not ones the public can use. But Supreme Court decisions and other information concerning the federal courts may be accessed on the Internet and at more than one address.

1. The New York Law Publishing Company, publisher of the *New York Law Journal* and the *National Law Journal*, has a very useful site for Supreme Court information:
http://www.ljextra/public/daily/ussup.html
The menu will lead you to:
News
Columns
U.S. Supreme Court (recent decisions)
U.S. Supreme Court (recent order lists)
U.S. Supreme Court Database (where you can search by key words)
NLJ Supreme Court Review (1993–94)
Biographies of the Supreme Court Justices
U.S. Supreme Court Press Releases
U.S. Supreme Court Proposed Revised Rules

2. The Legal Information Institute of Cornell Law School provides full texts of recent (1990–present) decisions and a selection of historic decisions as well. Cornell also offers you the capability of downloading all decisions issued since October 1995 in ASCII or WordPerfect 5.1 formats:
http://www.law.cornell.edu/supct
telnet://fatty.law.cornell.edu
  You can even browse the complete text of the U.S. Code at
http://www.law.cornell.edu/uscode
or access the latest Supreme Court Rules (or comment on the new proposed Rules) at
http://www.law.cornell.edu/rules

3. The Villanova Center for Information Law and Policy also has a very full menu worth checking out:
http://www.law.vill.edu
This home page menu includes The Federal Court Locator (**http://www.law.vill.edu/Fed-Ct/fedcourt. html**), which offers a map of the federal court system, links to Cornell for Supreme Court slip opinions, as well as to all circuit courts of appeals and related agencies including the Administrative Office of the U.S. Courts, the Federal Judicial Center, and the U.S. Department of Justice.

By the way, The Federal Web Locator, another menu choice of Villanova's home page, is an excellent way to link to just about all U.S. government Web sites. Another menu item, The State Court Locator, will link you to all state judiciaries on the Internet.

4. The Administrative Office of the U.S. Courts has set up a home page that they are attempting to make a "clearinghouse for information from and about the judicial branch of the U.S. government":
http://www.uscourts.gov
It includes press releases, vacancy lists for judges, and other goodies. However, one very important menu item will take you to a Directory of Electronic Public Access Services to Automated Information in the United States Federal Courts. This incredible directory is designed to "permit the public to gain direct, rapid and easy access to official court information and records from outside the courthouse." All you need is your modem and, in some cases, pocket change to contact almost every federal court in the land. (They are planning to change the "almost" to "every court" in the very near future.)

You can also read selected articles from *The Third Branch*, a monthly newsletter of the federal courts.

5. Another home page that may be useful is the one set up by the Federal Judicial Center—the federal courts' and related agencies, call up the home page created by the University City Republican Committee. The UCRC Guide can be found at

http://www.libertynet.org/~ucrc/uscourt/ federal.html

As of this writing it has enough to be useful, but is still being compiled.

9. A fascinating multimedia experience also awaits intrepid seekers after Supreme Court information. Northwestern University's Academic Technologies Department and the Northwestern University Library sponsor the unique Oyez, Oyez, Oyez: A Supreme Court WWW Resource.

http://Oyez.at.nwu.edu/oyez.html

The aim here is to provide information about major constitutional cases that reach the Supreme Court—and also to provide *digital recordings* of the Court's proceedings!

If your computer setup includes RealAudio software, you'll be able to access and *listen to* the actual oral arguments from selected cases from October 1955 onward. The audio collection even includes FDR's famous Fireside Chat about packing the Supreme Court. And you can also hear the voice of a marshal of the Court as he calls for the opening of courtroom business. Oyez!

6

Finding and
Identifying a Case

"IT LOOKS AS IF SMITHERS PACKAGING, VENDRELL
ET AL. VS. MELROSE COUNTY WATER SUPPLY IS
THE CLOSEST THING WE'LL GET ALL YEAR TO
A CRIME OF PASSION."

Whether in a brief, an article in a law review, or in a book such as this, when a case is mentioned there should also be a citation—a reference to its source. And if you're quoting from a case decision, the number of the page where the quoted material can be found should also be included. Armed with the citation, a reader who wishes to explore further can go to a law library or an on-line service and review the case.

Citations to Supreme Court cases give the first party to the case, followed by "v." (which stands for "versus" or "against"), followed by the name of the second party, followed by the reporter's (publication's) volume number, followed by the abbreviation used to indicate the reporter, followed by the first page of the case, followed by the page from which you are quoting, followed by the year of decision.

For example, a citation to the landmark abortion case would read *Roe v. Wade*, 410 U.S. 113 (1973). It tells you that the case of Roe, the plaintiff, against Wade, the defendant, can be found in volume 410 beginning at page 113 of *United States Reports* and that the Supreme Court's decision was handed down in 1973.

Other forms of citation tell you which court decided the case and whether the Supreme Court denied or granted certiorari, affirmed or reversed the lower court's decision, and more besides. For example, *United States v. Arnold, Schwinn & Co.*, 388 U.S. 365 (1967), *overruled in part by Continental T.V., Inc. v. GTE Sylvania, Inc.*, 433 U.S. 36 (1977); or *Alaska Airlines, Inc. v. United Airlines, Inc.*, 948 F.2d 536 (9th Cir. 1991), *cert. denied*, 112 S. Ct. 1603 (1992).

Supreme Court case decisions are found in the *United States Reports*, the official reporter, and published by the Government Printing Office. Other sources for Court decisions and opinions are: *United States Law Week* (U.S.L.W.), published by the Bureau of National Affairs; *Supreme Court Reporter* (S. Ct.), published by West Publishing Company; and the *United States Supreme Court Reports, Lawyers' Edition* (L. Ed. or L. Ed.2d), published by Lawyers Co-operative Publishing Company.

Until the *United States Reports* came into being in 1875, the official reports of the Supreme Court carried the name of the Court reporter.

Dallas (Dall.) 1789–1800
Cranch (Cranch or Cr.) 1801–1815
Wheaton (Wheat.) 1816–1827
Peters (Pet.) 1828–1842
Howard (How.) 1843–1860
Black (Black) 1861–1862
Wallace (Wall.) 1863–1874

The cases mentioned in this book are:

Alaska Airlines, Inc. v. United Airlines, Inc., 948 F.2d 536 (9th Cir. 1991), *cert. denied*, 112 S. Ct. 1603 (1992)

Betts v. Brady, 316 U.S. 455 (1942)

Brady v. United States, 397 U.S. 742 (1970)

Brown v. Board of Education of Topeka, 347 U.S. 483 (1954)

Chisholm v. Georgia, 2 Dall. 419 (1793)

Engel v. Vitale, 370 U.S. 421 (1962)

In re Gault, 387 U.S. 1 (1967)

Gibbons v. Ogden, 9 Wheat. 1 (1824)

Gideon v. Wainwright, 372 U.S. 335 (1963)

Griswold v. Connecticut, 381 U.S. 479 (1965)

Hartford Fire Insurance Co. et al. v. California et al., 113 S. Ct. 2891 (1993)

Hoyt v. Florida, 368 U.S. 57 (1961)

Illinois ex rel. McCollum v. Board of Education, 333 U.S. 293 (1948)

Johnson v. Zerbst, 304 U.S. 458 (1938)

Louisiana v. Mississippi, Docket 121, Orig. (decided October 31, 1995)

McNeil v. Wisconsin, 501 U.S. 171 (1991)

Mapp v. Ohio, 367 U.S. 643 (1961)

Marbury v. Madison, 1 Cranch 137 (1803)

Miranda v. Arizona, 384 U.S. 436 (1966)

Neal v. U.S., No. 94-9088 (decided Jan. 22, 1996)

New York Times Co. & Washington Post v. U.S., 403 U.S. 713 (1971)

Plessy v. Ferguson, 163 U.S. 537 (1896)

Roe v. Wade, 410 U.S. 683 (1973)

Rosenberg v. United States, 346 U.S. 273 (1953)

Siebold, Ex parte, 100 U.S. 371 (1880)

Smith v. Turner; Norris v. Boston, 7 How. 283 (1849)

Solem v. Helm, 462 U.S. 277 (1983)

Standard Oil Co. v. U.S., 221 U.S. 1 (1911)

Taylor v. Louisiana, 419 U.S. 522 (1975)

United States v. Arnold, Schwinn & Co., 388 U.S. 365 (1967), *overruled in part by Continental T.V., Inc. v. GTE Sylvania, Inc.*, 433 U.S. 36 (1977)

United States v. Eichman, 496 U.S. 310 (1990)

United States v. Nixon, 418 U.S. 683 (1974)

Ward's Cove Packing Co. v. Atonio, 490 U.S. 642 (1989)

judicial circuits, including the District of Columbia, and each circuit has a court of appeals. (There is also a thirteenth circuit, the Court of Appeals for the Federal Circuit, see below.) Each of the fifty states is assigned to one of the circuits; Puerto Rico, the Virgin Islands, Guam, and the Northern Mariana Islands are assigned variously to the first, third, and ninth circuits.

Circuit judges are nominated by the president and appointed with the advice and consent of the Senate. They hold their offices during good behavior as provided by Article III, section 1, of the Constitution. The senior judge, the judge who has served longest, who is under seventy years of age (sixty-five at the start of the term), has been in office at least one year, and has not previously been chief judge, serves as the chief judge of the circuit for a seven-year term.

One of the justices of the Supreme Court is assigned as circuit justice for each of the thirteen judicial circuits for emergency responses, and is responsible for such duties as issuing stays or injunctions.

Each court of appeals normally hears cases in panels consisting of three judges but may sit en banc ("with all judges present").

The judges of each circuit vote to determine the size of the judicial council for the circuit, which consists of the chief judge and an equal number of circuit and district judges. The council considers the state of federal judicial business in the circuit and may as stated in the U.S. Code, "make all necessary and appropriate orders for [its] effective and expeditious administration. . . ."

Once a year, the chief judge of each circuit summons a judicial conference of all circuit and district judges in the circuit, and sometimes members of the Bar, to discuss the business of the federal courts of the circuit.

The chief judge of each circuit also serves as a member of the Judicial Conference of the United States—the governing body for the administration of the federal judicial system as a whole.

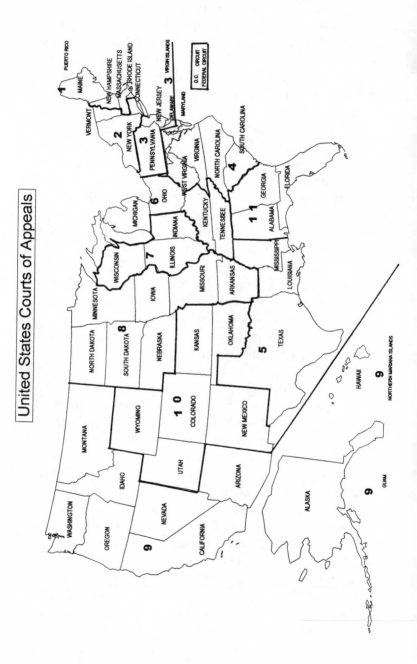

United States Courts of Appeals

THE UNITED STATES COURTS OF APPEALS, THEIR CIRCUIT
NUMBERS, THE DISTRICT COURTS BELOW THEM, AND THE
SUPREME COURT JUSTICES ASSIGNED TO THEM

District of Columbia Circuit
Washington, D.C.
Circuit Justice: Chief Justice William H. Rehnquist

First Circuit
Districts of Maine, New Hampshire, Massachusetts,
Rhode Island, and Puerto Rico
Circuit Justice: Justice David H. Souter

Second Circuit
Districts of Vermont, Connecticut, northern New York,
southern New York, eastern New York, and western
New York
Circuit Justice: Justice Ruth Bader Ginsburg

Third Circuit
Districts of New Jersey, eastern Pennsylvania, middle
Pennsylvania, western Pennsylvania, Delaware, and the
Virgin Islands
Circuit Justice: Justice David H. Souter

Fourth Circuit
Districts of Maryland, northern West Virginia, southern
West Virginia, eastern Virginia, western Virginia, eastern
North Carolina, middle North Carolina, western North
Carolina, and South Carolina
Circuit Justice: Chief Justice William H. Rehnquist

Fifth Circuit
Districts of northern Mississippi, southern Mississippi,
eastern Louisiana, middle Louisiana, western Louisiana, northern Texas, southern Texas, eastern Texas, and
western Texas
Circuit Justice: Justice Antonin Scalia

Sixth Circuit
Districts of northern Ohio, southern Ohio, eastern Michigan, western Michigan, eastern Kentucky, western Kentucky, eastern Tennessee, middle Tennessee, and western Tennessee
Circuit Justice: Justice John Paul Stevens

Seventh Circuit
Districts of northern Indiana, southern Indiana, northern Illinois, central Illinois, southern Illinois, eastern Wisconsin, and western Wisconsin
Circuit Justice: Justice John Paul Stevens

Eighth Circuit
Districts of Minnesota, northern Iowa, southern Iowa, eastern Missouri, western Missouri, eastern Arkansas, western Arkansas, Nebraska, North Dakota, and South Dakota
Circuit Justice: Justice Clarence Thomas

Ninth Circuit
Districts of northern California, eastern California, central California, southern California, Oregon, Nevada, Montana, eastern Washington, western Washington, Idaho, Arizona, Alaska, Hawaii, Territory of Guam, and the Northern Mariana Islands
Circuit Justice: Justice Sandra Day O'Connor

Tenth Circuit
Districts of Colorado, Wyoming, Utah, Kansas, eastern Oklahoma, western Oklahoma, northern Oklahoma, and New Mexico
Circuit Justice: Justice Stephen G. Breyer

Eleventh Circuit
Districts of northern Georgia, middle Georgia, southern Georgia, northern Florida, middle Florida, southern Flor-

ida, northern Alabama, middle Alabama, southern Alabama

Circuit Justice: Justice Anthony M. Kennedy

UNITED STATES COURT OF APPEALS
FOR THE FEDERAL CIRCUIT

This court was established by the Federal Courts Improvement Act of 1982 as successor to the former United States Court of Customs and Patent Appeals and the United States Court of Claims. The jurisdiction of the court is nationwide and includes appeals from the district courts in patent cases; appeals from the district courts in contract and certain other civil actions in which the United States is a defendant; and appeals from final decisions of the U.S. Court of International Trade, the U.S. Court of Federal Claims, and the U.S. Court of Veterans Appeals. The jurisdiction of the court also includes the review of administrative rulings by the Patent and Trademark Office, U.S. International Trade Commission, Secretary of Commerce, agency boards of contract appeals, and the Merit Systems Protection Board, as well as rulemaking of the Department of Veterans Affairs, review of decisions of the U.S. Senate Select Committee on Ethics concerning discrimination claims of Senate employees, and review of a final order of an entity to be designated by the president concerning discrimination claims of presidential appointees.

The court consists of twelve circuit judges. It sits in panels of three or more on each case and may also hear or rehear a case en banc. The court sits principally in Washington, D.C., but may hold court wherever any court of appeals sits.

Federal Circuit
Washington, D.C.
Circuit Justice: Chief Justice William H. Rehnquist

UNITED STATES COURT OF
MILITARY APPEALS

Subject only to certiorari review by the Supreme Court of the United States in a limited number of cases, this court serves as the final appellate tribunal to review court-martial convictions within all the armed services. It is exclusively an appellate criminal court, consisting of five civilian judges who are appointed for fifteen-year terms by the president with the advice and consent of the Senate.

The Federal Trial Courts

The lowest level of the federal court pyramid is made up of the trial courts. These include the district courts, the United States Tax Court, the United States Court of International Trade, the United States Court of Federal Claims, the United States Court of Veterans Appeals, and the Courts of Military Review.

UNITED STATES DISTRICT COURTS

The district courts are the trial courts of general federal jurisdiction. Each state has at least one district court; the larger states have as many as four. Altogether there are eighty-nine district courts in the fifty states, plus one in the District of Columbia. In addition, the Commonwealth of Puerto Rico has a district court, with jurisdiction corresponding to that of district courts in the various states.

At present, each district court has from 2 to 28 federal district judgeships, depending upon the amount of judicial work within its territory. Only one judge is usually required to hear and decide a case in a district court, but in some limited cases three judges are required to make up the court. The senior judge—the judge who's been there longest, who is under seventy years of age (sixty-five at inception of term), has been in office for at least one year, and has not previously been chief judge—serves as chief judge for a seven-year term. There are 610 permanent district judgeships in the fifty states, 15 in the District of Columbia and 7 in Puerto Rico.

District judges are nominated by the president and appointed with the advice and consent of the Senate. They hold their offices during good behavior as provided by Article III, section 1, of the Constitution. However, Congress may create temporary judgeships for a court that is overburdened, but it does so with the provision that when a vacancy occurs in that district, such vacancy shall not be filled. Each district court has one or more United States magistrate judges and bankruptcy judges, a clerk, a United States attorney, a United States marshal, probation officers, court reporters, and their staffs.

Cases from the district courts are reviewable on appeal by the applicable court of appeals. For example, if you lost your case in the district court of the northern district of California, you'd appeal it to the Court of Appeals for the Ninth Circuit.

TERRITORIAL COURTS

Congress has established district courts in the territories of Guam, the Virgin Islands, and in the Northern Mariana Islands, which presently is administered by the United States under a trusteeship agreement with the United Nations. These territorial courts have jurisdiction not only over the subjects described in the judicial article of the Constitution, but also over many local matters that, within the states, are decided in state courts. The District Court of Puerto Rico, by contrast, is established under Article III of the Constitution, is classified like other "district courts" and is called a "court of the United States."

There is one judge each in Guam and the Northern Mariana Islands, and two in the Virgin Islands. The judges in these courts are appointed for ten-year terms.

UNITED STATES TAX COURT

The Tax Court tries and adjudicates controversies involving the existence of deficiencies or overpayments in income, estate, gift, and generation–skipping transfer taxes in cases where deficiencies have been determined by the commissioner of internal revenue. It also hears cases commenced by transferees and fiduciaries who have been issued notices of liability by the commissioner.

The Tax Court has jurisdiction to redetermine excise taxes and penalties imposed on private foundations. Similar jurisdiction over excise taxes has been conferred with regard to public charities, qualified pension plans, and real estate investment trusts.

All decisions, other than small tax case decisions, are subject to review by the courts of appeals in the judicial circuit in which the case was initially tried, and thereafter by the Supreme Court of the United States upon the granting of a writ of certiorari.

The court is composed of nineteen judges. Its strength is augmented by senior judges, who may be recalled by the chief judge to perform further judicial duties, and by fourteen special trial judges, who are appointed by the chief judge and serve at the pleasure of the court. The chief judge is elected biennially from among the nineteen judges of the court.

The office of the court and all of its judges are located in Washington, D.C., with the exception of a field office located in Los Angeles, California. The court conducts trial sessions at various locations within the United States as reasonably convenient to taxpayers as practicable. Each trial session is conducted by a single judge or a special trial judge. All proceedings are public and are conducted judicially in accordance with the court's Rules of Practice and the rules of evidence applicable in trials without a jury in the U.S. District Court for the District of Columbia.

UNITED STATES COURT OF INTERNATIONAL TRADE

The Court of International Trade has all the powers in law and equity of a district court.

It has jurisdiction over any civil action against the United States arising from federal laws governing import transactions. This includes classification and valuation cases, as well as authority to review certain agency determinations under the Trade Agreements Act of 1979 involving antidumping and countervailing duty matters. In addition, it has exclusive jurisdiction of civil actions to review determinations as to the eligibility of workers, firms, and communities for adjustment assistance under the Trade Act of 1974. Civil actions commenced by the United States to recover customs duties, to recover on a customs bond, or for certain civil penalties alleging fraud or negligence are also within the exclusive jurisdiction of the court.

The court is composed of a chief judge and eight judges, not more than five of whom may belong to any one political party. Any of its judges may be temporarily designated and assigned by the chief justice of the United States Supreme Court to sit as a court of appeals or district court judge in any circuit or district. The court has a clerk and deputy clerks, a librarian, court reporters, and other supporting personnel.

Cases before the court may be tried before a jury. Under the Federal Courts Improvement Act of 1982, appeals are taken to the U.S. Court of Appeals for the Federal Circuit, and ultimately review may be sought in appropriate cases in the Supreme Court of the United States.

The principal offices are located in New York City, but the court can hear and determine cases arising at any port or place within the jurisdiction of the United States.

UNITED STATES COURT OF
FEDERAL CLAIMS

The court is composed of a chief judge, and fifteen associate judges. All judges are appointed for fifteen-year terms by the president with the advice and consent of the Senate.

The court has jurisdiction over claimants seeking money judgments against the United States. A claim must be founded upon either the United States Constitution; an act of Congress; the regulation of an executive department; an express or implied-in-fact contract with the United States; or damages, liquidated or unliquidated, in cases not associated with a tort.

The court also reports to Congress on bills referred by either the House of Representatives or the Senate.

Judgments of the court are final and conclusive on both the claimant and the United States. All judgments are subject to appeal to the United States Court of Appeals for the Federal Circuit, and a loss there can be appealed to the Supreme Court. Collateral to any judgment, the court can issue orders directing the restoration to office or status of any claimant, or the correction of applicable records.

The court's jurisdiction is nationwide. Trials are conducted before individual judges at locations most convenient and least expensive to citizens.

UNITED STATES COURT OF
VETERANS APPEALS

The United States Court of Veterans Appeals was established on November 18, 1988, and given exclusive jurisdiction to review decisions of the Board of Veterans Appeals. However, the court cannot review the schedule of ratings for disabilities or actions of the secretary in adopting or revising that schedule.

Decisions of the Court of Veterans Appeals may be appealed to the United States Court of Appeals for the

Federal Circuit. If necessary, they may be further appealed to the Supreme Court.

The court consists of a chief judge and at least two, but not more than six, associate judges. All judges are appointed by the president with the advice and consent of the Senate for a term of fifteen years.

The court's principal office is in the District of Columbia, but the court can also act at any place within the United States.

COURTS OF MILITARY REVIEW

Decisions of Army, Navy–Marine Corps, Air Force, and Coast Guard Courts of Military Review may be appealed to the United States Court of Military Appeals. Failing there, they may be appealed to the Supreme Court.

Appendix B:
Supreme Court Justices

Table 1. Associate Justices

Justice	Years on Court	President Who Nominated	Party	Senate Majority
John Rutledge	1789–1791	George Washington	F	Pro-Admin.
William Cushing	1789–1810	George Washington	F	Pro-Admin.
James Wilson	1789–1798	George Washington	F	Pro-Admin.
John Blair	1789–1796	George Washington	F	Pro-Admin.

Justice	Years on Court	President Who Nominated	Party	Senate Majority
James Iredell	1790–1799	George Washington	F	Pro-Admin.
Thomas Johnson	1791–1793	George Washington	F	Pro-Admin.
William Paterson	1793–1806	George Washington	F	Pro-Admin.
Samuel Chase	1796–1811	George Washington	F	R
Bushrod Washington	1798–1829	John Adams	F	R
Alfred Moore	1799–1804	John Adams	F	R
William Johnson	1804–1834	Thomas Jefferson	D-R	F
Henry B. Livingston	1806–1823	Thomas Jefferson	D-R	F
Thomas Todd	1807–1826	Thomas Jefferson	D-R	F
Gabriel Duval	1811–1835	James Madison	D-R	F
Joseph Story	1811–1845	James Madison	D-R	F
Smith Thompson	1823–1843	James Monroe	D-R	R
Robert Trimble	1826–1828	John Adams	D-R	Adams
John McLean	1829–1861	Andrew Jackson	D	J
Henry Baldwin	1830–1844	Andrew Jackson	D	AJ
James M. Wayne	1835–1867	Andrew Jackson	D	AJ
Philip P. Barbour	1836–1841	Andrew Jackson	D	AJ
John Catron*	1837–1865	Andrew Jackson	D	D
John McKinley	1837–1852	Martin Van Buren	D	D
Peter V. Daniel	1841–1860	Martin Van Buren	D	D
Samuel Nelson	1845–1872	John Tyler	W	W
Levy Woodbury	1845–1851	James K. Polk	D	D
Robert C. Grier	1846–1870	James K. Polk	D	D
Benjamin R. Curtis	1851–1857	Millard Fillmore	W	D
John A. Campbell	1853–1861	Franklin Pierce	D	D
Nathan Clifford	1858–1881	James Buchanan	D	D
Noah H. Swayne	1862–1881	Abraham Lincoln	R	R
Samuel F. Miller	1862–1890	Abraham Lincoln	R	R
David Davis	1862–1877	Abraham Lincoln	R	R
Stephen J. Field	1863–1897	Abraham Lincoln	R	R
William Strong	1870–1880	Ulysses S. Grant	R	R
Joseph P. Bradley	1870–1892	Ulysses S. Grant	R	R
Ward Hunt	1873–1882	Ulysses S. Grant	R	R
John M. I. Harlan	1877–1911	Rutherford B. Hayes	R	R
William B. Woods	1881–1887	Rutherford B. Hayes	R	D
Stanley Matthews	1881–1889	James A. Garfield	R	R

Justice	*Years on Court*	*President Who Nominated*	*Party*	*Senate Majority*
Horace Gray	1882–1902	Chester A. Arthur	R	R
Samuel Blatchford	1882–1893	Chester A. Arthur	R	R
Lucius Q. C. Lamar	1888–1893	Grover Cleveland	D	R
David J. Brewer	1889–1910	Benjamin Harrison	R	R
Henry B. Brown	1891–1906	Benjamin Harrison	R	R
George Shiras, Jr.	1892–1903	Benjamin Harrison	R	R
Howell E. Jackson	1893–1895	Benjamin Harrison	R	R
Edward D. White	1894–1910	Grover Cleveland	D	D
Rufus W. Peckham	1896–1909	Grover Cleveland	D	R
Joseph McKenna	1898–1925	William McKinley	R	R
Oliver W. Holmes, Jr.	1902–1932	Theodore Roosevelt	R	R
William R. Day	1903–1922	Theodore Roosevelt	R	R
William H. Moody	1906–1910	Theodore Roosevelt	R	R
Horace Lurton	1910–1914	William H. Taft	R	R
Charles E. Hughes	1910–1916	William H. Taft	R	R
Willis Van Devanter	1911–1937	William H.Taft	R	R
Joseph R. Lamar	1911–1916	William H. Taft	R	R
Mahlon Pitney	1912–1922	William H. Taft	R	R
James C. McReynolds	1914–1941	Woodrow Wilson	D	D
Louis D. Brandeis	1916–1939	Woodrow Wilson	D	D
John H. Clarke	1916–1922	Woodrow Wilson	D	D
George Sutherland	1922–1938	Warren G. Harding	R	R
Pierce Butler	1923–1939	Warren G. Harding	R	R
Edward T. Sanford	1923–1930	Warren G. Harding	R	R
Harlan F. Stone	1925–1941	Calvin Coolidge	R	R
Owen J. Roberts	1930–1945	Herbert Hoover	R	R
Benjamin N. Cardozo	1932–1938	Herbert Hoover	R	R
Hugo L. Black	1937–1971	Franklin D. Roosevelt	D	D
Stanley F. Reed	1938–1957	Franklin D. Roosevelt	D	D
Felix Frankfurter	1939–1962	Franklin D. Roosevelt	D	D
William O. Douglas	1939–1975	Franklin D. Roosevelt	D	D
Frank Murphy	1940–1949	Franklin D. Roosevelt	D	D
James F. Byrnes	1941–1942	Franklin D. Roosevelt	D	D
Robert H. Jackson	1941–1954	Franklin D. Roosevelt	D	D
Wiley B. Rutledge	1943–1949	Franklin D. Roosevelt	D	D
Harold H. Burton	1945–1958	Harry S. Truman	D	D

Table 3. Nominees Who Did Not Make It

Nominee	Year	President Who Proposed	Party	Action Taken	Senate Majority
John Rutledge★★	1795	George Washington	F	withdrawn	Pro-Admin
Alexander Wolcott	1811	James Madison	D-R	rejected	F
John Crittenden	1828	John Adams	D-R	none★★★	J
Roger B. Taney★	1835	Andrew Jackson	D	none	J
John Spencer	1844	John Tyler	W	rejected	W
Reuben Walworth	1844	John Tyler	W	withdrawn	W
Edward King	1844	John Tyler	W	none	W
Edward King★	1845	John Tyler	W	withdrawn	W
John Read	1845	John Tyler	W	none	D
George Woodward	1845	James K. Polk	D	rejected	D
Edward Bradford	1852	Millard Fillmore	W	none	D
George Badger	1853	Millard Fillmore	W	none	D
William Micou	1853	Millard Fillmore	W	none	D
Jeremiah Black	1861	James Buchanan	D	rejected	D
Henry Stanberry	1866	Andrew Johnson	W	none	R
Ebenezer Hoar	1869	Ulysses S. Grant	R	rejected	R
George Williams	1873	Ulysses S. Grant	R	withdrawn	R
Caleb Cushing	1874	Ulysses S. Grant	R	withdrawn	R
Stanley Matthews★	1881	Rutherford B. Hayes	R	none	D
William Hornblower	1893	Grover Cleveland	D	rejected	D
Wheeler Peckham	1894	Grover Cleveland	D	rejected	D
John Parker	1930	Herbert Hoover	R	rejected	R
Abe Fortas★	1968	Lyndon B. Johnson	D	rejected	D
Homer Thornberry	1968	Lyndon B. Johnson	D	none	D
Clement Haynsworth	1969	Richard M. Nixon	R	rejected	D
G. Harold Carswell	1970	Richard M. Nixon	R	rejected	D
Robert Bork	1987	Ronald Reagan	R	rejected	D
Douglas Ginsburg	1987	Ronald Reagan	R	withdrawn	D

★ Taney and Matthews were renominated and confirmed. King was nominated a second time and President Tyler was forced to withdraw his name. Fortas, a sitting Justice, was rejected when nominated for chief justice.

★★ Presided over Court without confirmation Aug.–Dec. while Congress was in recess. Senate refused to confirm.

★★★ When the Senate takes no action on a nomination, the candidate is in reality rejected.

D=Democrat;   D-R=Democrat-Republican;   Pro-Admin.=Pro-Administration;
R=Republican;   W=Whig

Appendix C:
The Rules of the
Supreme Court of
the United States

"I BEG YOUR PARDON, YOUNG MAN, BUT WE
GIVE OUR OWN DISSENTING OPINIONS."

Part I. The Court
Rule 1. Clerk

1. The Clerk receives documents for filing with the Court and
   has authority to reject any submitted filing that does not
   comply with these Rules.

2. The Clerk maintains the Court's records and will not permit any of them to be removed from the Court building except as authorized by the Court. Any document filed with the Clerk and made a part of the Court's records may not thereafter be withdrawn from the official Court files. After the conclusion of proceedings in this Court, original records and documents transmitted to this Court by any other court will be returned to the court from which they were received.

3. Unless the Court or the Chief Justice orders otherwise, the Clerk's office is open from 9 A.M. to 5 P.M., Monday through Friday, except on federal legal holidays listed in 5 U.S.C. § 6103.

Rule 2. Library

1. The Court's library is available for use by appropriate personnel of this Court, members of the Bar of this Court, Members of Congress and their legal staffs, and attorneys for the United States and for federal departments and agencies.

2. The library's hours are governed by regulations made by the Librarian with the approval of the Chief Justice or the Court.

3. Library books may not be removed from the Court building, except by a Justice or a member of a Justice's staff.

Rule 3. Term

The Court holds a continuous annual Term commencing on the first Monday in October and ending on the day before the first Monday in October of the following year. See 28 U.S.C. § 2. At the end of each Term, all cases pending on the docket are continued to the next Term.

Rule 4. Sessions and Quorum

1. Open sessions of the Court are held beginning at 10 A.M. on the first Monday in October of each year, and thereafter as

announced by the Court. Unless it orders otherwise, the Court sits to hear arguments from 10 A.M. until noon and from 1 P.M. until 3 P.M.

2. Six Members of the Court constitute a quorum. See 28 U.S.C. § 1. In the absence of a quorum on any day appointed for holding a session of the Court, the Justices attending—or if no Justice is present, the Clerk or a Deputy Clerk—may announce that the Court will not meet until there is a quorum.

3. When appropriate, the Court will direct the Clerk or the Marshal to announce recesses.

Rule 5. Admission to the Bar

1. To qualify for admission to the Bar of this Court, an applicant must have been admitted to practice in the highest court of a State, Commonwealth, Territory or Possession, or the District of Columbia for a period of at least three years immediately before the date of application; must not have been the subject of any adverse disciplinary action pronounced or in effect during that 3-year period; and must appear to the Court to be of good moral and professional character.

2. Each applicant shall file with the Clerk (1) a certificate from the presiding judge, clerk, or other authorized official of that court evidencing the applicant's admission to practice there and the applicant's current good standing, and (2) a completely executed copy of the form approved by this Court and furnished by the Clerk containing (a) the applicant's personal statement, and (b) the statement of two sponsors endorsing the correctness of the applicant's statement, stating that the applicant possesses all the qualifications required for admission, and affirming that the applicant is of good moral and professional character. Both sponsors must be members of the Bar of this Court who personally know, but are not related to, the applicant.

3. If the documents submitted demonstrate that the applicant possesses the necessary qualifications, and if the applicant has

signed the oath or affirmation and paid the required fee, the Clerk will notify the applicant of acceptance by the Court as a member of the Bar and issue a certificate of admission. An applicant who so wishes may be admitted in open court on oral motion by a member of the Bar of this Court, provided that all other requirements for admission have been satisfied.

4. Each applicant shall sign the following oath or affirmation: I, _____, do solemnly swear (or affirm) that as an attorney and as a counselor of this Court, I will conduct myself uprightly and according to law, and that I will support the Constitution of the United States.

5. The fee for admission to the Bar and a certificate bearing the seal of the Court is $100, payable to the United States Supreme Court. The Marshal will deposit such fees in a separate fund to be disbursed by the Marshal at the direction of the Chief Justice for the costs of admissions, for the benefit of the Court and its Bar, and for related purposes.

6. The fee for a duplicate certificate of admission to the Bar bearing the seal of the Court is $15, payable to the United States Supreme Court. The proceeds will be maintained by the Marshal as provided in paragraph 5 of this Rule.

Part II. Attorneys and Counselors
Rule 6. Argument *Pro Hac Vice*

1. An attorney not admitted to practice in the highest court of a State, Commonwealth, Territory or Possession, or the District of Columbia for the requisite three years, but otherwise eligible for admission to practice in this Court under Rule 5.1, may be permitted to argue *pro hac vice*.

2. An attorney qualified to practice in the courts of a foreign state may be permitted to argue *pro hac vice*.

3. Oral argument *pro hac vice* is allowed only on motion of the counsel of record for the party on whose behalf leave is requested. The motion shall state concisely the qualifications of the attorney who is to argue *pro hac vice*. It shall be filed with the Clerk, in the form required by Rule 21, no later than the date on which the respondent's or appellee's brief on the

merits is due to be filed and it shall be accompanied by proof of service as required by Rule 29.

Rule 7. Prohibition Against Practice

No employee of this Court shall practice as an attorney or counselor in any court or before any agency of government while employed by the Court; nor shall any person after leaving such employment participate in any professional capacity in any case pending before this Court or in any case being considered for filing in this Court, until two years have elapsed after separation; nor shall a former employee ever participate in any professional capacity in any case that was pending in this Court during the employee's tenure.

Rule 8. Disbarment and Disciplinary Action

1. Whenever a member of the Bar of this Court has been disbarred or suspended from practice in any court of record, or has engaged in conduct unbecoming a member of the Bar of this Court, the Court will enter an order suspending that member from practice before this Court and affording the member an opportunity to show cause, within 40 days, why a disbarment order should not be entered. Upon response, or if no response is timely filed, the Court will enter an appropriate order.

2. After reasonable notice and an opportunity to show cause why disciplinary action should not be taken, and after a hearing if material facts are in dispute, the Court may take any appropriate disciplinary action against any attorney who is admitted to practice before it for conduct unbecoming a member of the Bar or for failure to comply with these Rules or any Rule or order of the Court.

Rule 9. Appearance of Counsel

1. An attorney seeking to file a document in this Court in a representative capacity must first be admitted to practice be-

fore this Court as provided in Rule 5, except that admission to the Bar of this Court is not required for an attorney appointed under the Criminal Justice Act of 1964, see 18 U.S.C. § 3006A(d)(6), or under any other applicable federal statute. The attorney whose name, address, and telephone number appear on the cover of a document presented for filing is considered counsel of record, and a separate notice of appearance need not be filed. If the name of more than one attorney is shown on the cover of the document, the attorney who is counsel of record shall be clearly identified.

2. An attorney representing a party who will not be filing a document shall enter a separate notice of appearance as counsel of record indicating the name of the party represented. A separate notice of appearance shall also be entered whenever an attorney is substituted as counsel of record in a particular case.

Part III. Jurisdiction on Writ of Certiorari
Rule 10. Considerations Governing Review on Writ of Certiorari

Review on a writ of certiorari is not a matter of right, but of judicial discretion. A petition for a writ of certiorari will be granted only for compelling reasons. The following, although neither controlling nor fully measuring the Court's discretion, indicate the character of the reasons the Court considers:

(a) a United States court of appeals has entered a decision in conflict with the decision of another United States court of appeals on the same important matter; has decided an important federal question in a way that conflicts with a decision by a state court of last resort; or has so far departed from the accepted and usual course of judicial proceedings, or sanctioned such a departure by a lower court, as to call for an exercise of this Court's supervisory power;

(b) a state court of last resort has decided an important federal question in a way that conflicts with the deci-

sion of another state court of last resort or of a United
States court of appeals;

(c) a state court or a United States court of appeals has decided an important question of federal law that has not
been, but should be, settled by this Court, or has decided an important federal question in a way that conflicts with relevant decisions of this Court.

A petition for a writ of certiorari is rarely granted when the asserted error consists of erroneous factual findings or the misappli-
cation of a properly stated rule of law.

Rule 11. Certiorari to a United States Court of Appeals before Judgment

A petition for a writ of certiorari to review a case pending in a
United States court of appeals, before judgment is entered in
that court, will be granted only upon a showing that the case is
of such imperative public importance as to justify deviation from
normal appellate practice and to require immediate determination in this Court. See 28 U.S.C. § 2101(e).

Rule 12. Review on Certiorari: How Sought; Parties

1. Except as provided in paragraph 2 of this Rule, the petitioner
   shall file 40 copies of a petition for a writ of certiorari, prepared as required by Rule 33.1, and shall pay the Rule 38(a)
   docket fee.

2. A petitioner proceeding *in forma pauperis* under Rule 39 shall
   file an original and 10 copies of a petition for a writ of certiorari prepared as required by Rule 33.2, together with an
   original and 10 copies of the motion for leave to proceed *in
   forma pauperis*. A copy of the motion shall precede and be attached to each copy of the petition. An inmate confined in
   an institution, if proceeding *in forma pauperis* and not represented by counsel, need file only an original petition and
   motion.

3. Whether prepared under Rule 33.1 or Rule 33.2, the petition shall comply in all respects with Rule 14 and shall be submitted with proof of service as required by Rule 29. The case then will be placed on the docket. It is the petitioner's duty to notify all respondents promptly, on a form supplied by the Clerk, of the date of filing, the date the case was placed on the docket, and the docket number of the case. The notice shall be served as required by Rule 29.

4. Parties interested jointly, severally, or otherwise in a judgment may petition separately for a writ of certiorari; or any two or more may join in a petition. A party not shown on the petition as joined therein at the time the petition is filed may not later join in that petition. When two or more judgments are sought to be reviewed on a writ of certiorari to the same court and involve identical or closely related questions, a single petition for a writ of certiorari covering all the judgments suffices. A petition for a writ of certiorari may not be joined with any other pleading, except that any motion for leave to proceed *in forma pauperis* shall be attached.

5. No more than 30 days after a case has been placed on the docket, a respondent seeking to file a conditional cross-petition (i.e., a cross-petition that otherwise would be untimely) shall file, with proof of service as required by Rule 29, 40 copies of the cross-petition prepared as required by Rule 33.1, except that a cross-petitioner proceeding *in forma pauperis* under Rule 39 shall comply with Rule 12.2. The cross-petition shall comply in all respects with this Rule and Rule 14, except that material already reproduced in the appendix to the opening petition need not be reproduced again. A cross-petitioning respondent shall pay the Rule 38(a) docket fee or submit a motion for leave to proceed *in forma pauperis*. The cover of the cross-petition shall indicate clearly that it is a conditional cross-petition. The cross-petition then will be placed on the docket, subject to the provisions of Rule 13.4. It is the cross-petitioner's duty to notify all cross respondents promptly, on a form supplied by the Clerk, of the date of filing, the date the cross-petition was placed on the docket, and the docket number of the cross-petition. The notice shall be

served as required by Rule 29. A cross-petition for a writ of certiorari may not be joined with any other pleading, except that any motion for leave to proceed *in forma pauperis* shall be attached. The time to file a cross-petition will not be extended.

6. All parties to the proceeding in the court whose judgment is sought to be reviewed are deemed parties entitled to file documents in this Court, unless the petitioner notifies the Clerk of this Court in writing of the petitioner's belief that one or more of the parties below have no interest in the outcome of the petition. A copy of such notice shall be served as required by Rule 29 on all parties to the proceeding below. A party noted as no longer interested may remain a party by notifying the Clerk promptly, with service on the other parties, of an intention to remain a party. All parties other than the petitioner are considered respondents, but any respondent who supports the position of a petitioner shall meet the petitioner's time schedule for filing documents, except that a response supporting the petition shall be filed within 20 days after the case is placed on the docket, and that time will not be extended. Parties who file no document will not qualify for any relief from this Court.

7. The clerk of the court having possession of the record shall keep it until notified by the Clerk of this Court to certify and transmit it. In any document filed with this Court, a party may cite or quote from the record, even if it has not been transmitted to this Court. When requested by the Clerk of this Court to certify and transmit the record, or any part of it, the clerk of the court having possession of the record shall number the documents to be certified and shall transmit therewith a numbered list specifically identifying each document transmitted. If the record, or stipulated portions, have been printed for the use of the court below, that printed record, plus the proceedings in the court below, may be certified as the record unless one of the parties or the Clerk of this Court requests otherwise. The record may consist of certified copies, but if the lower court is of the view that original documents of any kind should be seen by this Court, that

court may provide by order for the transport, safekeeping, and return of such originals.

Rule 13. Review on Certiorari: Time for Petitioning

1. Unless otherwise provided by law, a petition for a writ of certiorari to review a judgment in any case, civil or criminal, entered by a state court of last resort or a United States court of appeals (including the United States Court of Appeals for the Armed Forces) is timely when it is filed with the Clerk of this Court within 90 days after entry of the judgment. A petition for a writ of certiorari seeking review of a judgment of a lower state court that is subject to discretionary review by the state court of last resort is timely when it is filed with the Clerk within 90 days after entry of the order denying discretionary review.

2. The Clerk will not file any petition for a writ of certiorari that is jurisdictionally out of time. See, e.g., 28 U.S.C. § 2101(c).

3. The time to file a petition for a writ of certiorari runs from the date of entry of the judgment or order sought to be reviewed, and not from the issuance date of the mandate (or its equivalent under local practice). But if a petition for rehearing is timely filed in the lower court by any party, the time to file the petition for a writ of certiorari for all parties (whether or not they requested rehearing or joined in the petition for rehearing) runs from the date of the denial of the petition for rehearing or, if the petition for rehearing is granted, the subsequent entry of judgment. A suggestion made to a United States court of appeals for a rehearing en banc is not a petition for rehearing within the meaning of this Rule unless so treated by the United States court of appeals.

4. A cross-petition for a writ of certiorari is timely when it is filed with the Clerk as provided in paragraphs 1, 3, and 5 of this Rule, or in Rule 12.5. However, a conditional cross-petition (which except for Rule 12.5 would be untimely)

will not be granted unless another party's timely petition for a writ of certiorari is granted.

5. For good cause, a Justice may extend the time to file a petition for a writ of certiorari for a period not exceeding 60 days. An application to extend the time to file shall set out the basis for jurisdiction in this Court, identify the judgment sought to be reviewed, include a copy of the opinion and any order respecting rehearing, and set out specific reasons why an extension of time is justified. The application must be received by the Clerk at least 10 days before the date the petition is due, except in extraordinary circumstances. For the time and manner of presenting the application, see Rules 21, 22, 30, and 33.2. An application to extend the time to file a petition for a writ of certiorari is not favored.

Rule 14. Content of a Petition for a Writ of Certiorari

1. A petition for a writ of certiorari shall contain, in the order indicated:

    (a) The questions presented for review, expressed concisely in relation to the circumstances of the case, without unnecessary detail. The questions should be short and should not be argumentative or repetitive. If the petitioner or respondent is under a death sentence that may be affected by the disposition of the petition, the notation "capital case" shall precede the questions presented. The questions shall be set out on the first page following the cover, and no other information may appear on that page. The statement of any question presented is deemed to comprise every subsidiary question fairly included therein. Only the questions set out in the petition, or fairly included therein, will be considered by the Court.

    (b) A list of all parties to the proceeding in the court whose judgment is sought to be reviewed (unless the caption of the case contains the names of all the parties), and a list of parent companies and nonwholly owned subsidiaries as required by Rule 29.6.

(c) If the petition exceeds five pages, a table of contents and a table of cited authorities.

(d) Citations of the official and unofficial reports of the opinions and orders entered in the case by courts or administrative agencies.

(e) A concise statement of the basis for jurisdiction in this Court, showing:

  i. the date the judgment or order sought to be reviewed was entered (and, if applicable, a statement that the petition is filed under this Court's Rule 11);

  ii. the date of any order respecting rehearing, and the date and terms of any order granting an extension of time to file the petition for a writ of certiorari;

  iii. express reliance on Rule 12.5, when a cross-petition for a writ of certiorari is filed under that Rule, and the date of docketing of the petition for a writ of certiorari in connection with which the cross-petition is filed;

  iv. the statutory provision believed to confer on this Court jurisdiction to review on a writ of certiorari the judgment or order in question; and

  v. if applicable, a statement that the notifications required by Rule 29.4(b) or (c) have been made.

(f) The constitutional provisions, treaties, statutes, ordinances, and regulations involved in the case, set out verbatim with appropriate citation. If the provisions involved are lengthy, their citation alone suffices at this point, and their pertinent text shall be set out in the appendix referred to in subparagraph 1(i).

(g) A concise statement of the case setting out the facts material to consideration of the questions presented, and also containing the following:

  i. If review of a state-court judgment is sought, specification of the stage in the proceedings, both in the court of first instance and in the appellate courts, when the federal questions sought to be reviewed were raised; the method or manner of raising them and the way in which they were passed on by those courts; and pertinent quotations of specific portions of the record or summary thereof, with specific reference to the places in the record where the matter appears (e.g., court opinion, ruling on exception, portion of court's charge and exception thereto, assignment of error), so as to show that the federal question was timely and properly raised and that this Court has jurisdiction to review the judgment on a writ of certiorari. When the portions of the record relied on under this subparagraph are voluminous, they shall be included in the appendix referred to in subparagraph 1(i).

ii. If review of a judgment of a United States court of appeals is sought, the basis for federal jurisdiction in the court of first instance.

(h) A direct and concise argument amplifying the reasons relied on for allowance of the writ. See Rule 10.

(i) An appendix containing, in the order indicated:

i. the opinions, orders, findings of fact, and conclusions of law, whether written or orally given and transcribed, entered in conjunction with the judgment sought to be reviewed;

ii. any other opinions, orders, findings of fact, and conclusions of law entered in the case by courts or administrative agencies, and, if reference thereto is necessary to ascertain the grounds of the judgment, of those in companion cases (each document shall include the caption showing the name of the issuing court or agency, the title and number of the case, and the date of entry);

iii. any order on rehearing, including the caption showing the name of the issuing court, the title and number of the case, and the date of entry;

iv. the judgment sought to be reviewed if the date of its entry is different from the date of the opin-

ion or order required in sub subparagraph (i) of
this subparagraph;

    v. material required by subparagraphs 1(f) or 1(g)(i);
and

   vi. any other material the petitioner believes essential
to understand the petition.

If the material required by this subparagraph is voluminous, it
may be presented in a separate volume or volumes with appropriate covers.

2. All contentions in support of a petition for a writ of certiorari
shall be set out in the body of the petition, as provided in
subparagraph 1(h) of this Rule. No separate brief in support
of a petition for a writ of certiorari may be filed, and the
Clerk will not file any petition for a writ of certiorari to
which any supporting brief is annexed or appended.

3. A petition for a writ of certiorari should be stated briefly and
in plain terms and may not exceed the page limitations specified in Rule 33.

4. The failure of a petitioner to present with accuracy, brevity,
and clarity whatever is essential to ready and adequate understanding of the points requiring consideration is sufficient reason for the Court to deny a petition.

5. If the Clerk determines that a petition submitted timely and
in good faith is in a form that does not comply with this
Rule or with Rule 33 or Rule 34, the Clerk will return it
with a letter indicating the deficiency. A corrected petition
received no more than 60 days after the date of the Clerk's
letter will be deemed timely.

Rule 15. Briefs in Opposition; Reply Briefs; Supplemental Briefs

1. A brief in opposition to the petition for a writ of certiorari
may be filed by the respondent in any case, but is not mandatory except in a capital case, see Rule 14.1(a) or when ordered by the Court.

2. A brief in opposition should be stated briefly and in plain
terms and may not exceed the page limitations specified in

whose judgment is to be reviewed. The case then will be scheduled for briefing and oral argument. If the record has not previously been filed in this Court, the Clerk will request the clerk of the court having possession of the record to certify and transmit it. A formal writ will not issue unless specially directed.

3. Whenever the Court denies a petition for a writ of certiorari, the Clerk will prepare, sign, and enter an order to that effect and will notify forthwith counsel of record and the court whose judgment was sought to be reviewed. The order of denial will not be suspended pending disposition of a petition for rehearing except by order of the Court or a Justice.

Part IV. Other Jurisdiction
Rule 17. Procedure in an Original Action

1. This Rule applies only to an action invoking the Court's original jurisdiction under Article III of the Constitution of the United States. See also 28 U.S.C. § 1251 and U. S. Const., Amdt. 11. A petition for an extraordinary writ in aid of the Court's appellate jurisdiction shall be filed as provided in Rule 20.

2. The form of pleadings and motions prescribed by the Federal Rules of Civil Procedure is followed. In other respects, those Rules and the Federal Rules of Evidence may be taken as guides.

3. The initial pleading shall be preceded by a motion for leave to file, and may be accompanied by a brief in support of the motion. Forty copies of each document shall be filed, with proof of service. Service shall be as required by Rule 29, except that when an adverse party is a State, service shall be made on both the Governor and the Attorney General of that State.

4. The case will be placed on the docket when the motion for leave to file and the initial pleading are filed with the Clerk. The Rule 38(a) docket fee shall be paid at that time.

5. No more than 60 days after receiving the motion for leave to file and the initial pleading, an adverse party shall file 40 cop-

ies of any brief in opposition to the motion, with proof of service as required by Rule 29. The Clerk will distribute the filed documents to the Court for its consideration upon receiving an express waiver of the right to file a brief in opposition, or, if no waiver or brief is filed, upon the expiration of the time allowed for filing. If a brief in opposition is timely filed, the Clerk will distribute the filed documents to the Court for its consideration no less than 10 days after the brief in opposition is filed. A reply brief may be filed, but consideration of the case will not be deferred pending its receipt. The Court thereafter may grant or deny the motion, set it for oral argument, direct that additional documents be filed, or require that other proceedings be conducted.

6. A summons issued out of this Court shall be served on the defendant 60 days before the return day specified therein. If the defendant does not respond by the return day, the plaintiff may proceed *ex parte.*

7. Process against a State issued out of this Court shall be served on both the Governor and the Attorney General of that State.

Rule 18. Appeal from a United States District Court

1. When a direct appeal from a decision of a United States district court is authorized by law, the appeal is commenced by filing a notice of appeal with the clerk of the district court within the time provided by law after entry of the judgment sought to be reviewed. The time to file may not be extended. The notice of appeal shall specify the parties taking the appeal, designate the judgment, or part thereof, appealed from and the date of its entry, and specify the statute or statutes under which the appeal is taken. A copy of the notice of appeal shall be served on all parties to the proceeding as required by Rule 29, and proof of service shall be filed in the district court together with the notice of appeal.

2. All parties to the proceeding in the district court are deemed parties entitled to file documents in this Court, but a party having no interest in the outcome of the appeal may so

notify the Clerk of this Court and shall serve a copy of
the notice on all other parties. Parties interested jointly,
severally, or otherwise in the judgment may appeal separately, or any two or more may join in an appeal. When
two or more judgments involving identical or closely related
questions are sought to be reviewed on appeal from the
same court, a notice of appeal for each judgment shall be
filed with the clerk of the district court, but a single jurisdictional statement covering all the judgments suffices. Parties who file no document will not qualify for any relief
from this Court.

3. No more than 60 days after filing the notice of appeal in
the district court, the appellant shall file 40 copies of a jurisdictional statement and shall pay the Rule 38 docket fee,
except that an appellant proceeding *in forma pauperis* under
Rule 39, including an inmate of an institution, shall file the
number of copies required for a petition by such a person
under Rule 12.2, together with a motion for leave to proceed *in forma pauperis*, a copy of which shall precede and be
attached to each copy of the jurisdictional statement. The
jurisdictional statement shall follow, insofar as applicable, the
form for a petition for a writ of certiorari prescribed by
Rule 14, and shall be served as required by Rule 29. The
appendix shall include a copy of the notice of appeal showing the date it was filed in the district court. For good
cause, a Justice may extend the time to file a jurisdictional
statement for a period not exceeding 60 days. An application
to extend the time to file a jurisdictional statement shall set
out the basis for jurisdiction in this Court; identify the judgment sought to be reviewed; include a copy of the opinion,
any order respecting rehearing, and the notice of appeal; and
set out specific reasons why an extension of time is justified.
For the time and manner of presenting the application, see
Rules 21, 22, and 30. An application to extend the time to
file a jurisdictional statement is not favored.

4. No more than 30 days after a case has been placed on the
docket, an appellee seeking to file a conditional cross-appeal

(i.e., a cross-appeal that otherwise would be untimely) shall file, with proof of service as required by Rule 29, a jurisdictional statement that complies in all respects (including number of copies filed) with paragraph 3 of this Rule, except that material already reproduced in the appendix to the opening jurisdictional statement need not be reproduced again. A cross-appealing appellee shall pay the Rule 38 docket fee or submit a motion for leave to proceed *in forma pauperis*. The cover of the cross-appeal shall indicate clearly that it is a conditional cross-appeal. The cross-appeal then will be placed on the docket. It is the cross-appellant's duty to notify all cross-appellees promptly, on a form supplied by the Clerk, of the date of filing, the date the cross-appeal was placed on the docket, and the docket number of the cross-appeal. The notice shall be served as required by Rule 29. A cross-appeal may not be joined with any other pleading, except that any motion for leave to proceed *in forma pauperis* shall be attached. The time to file a cross-appeal will not be extended.

5. After a notice of appeal has been filed in the district court, but before the case is placed on this Court's docket, the parties may dismiss the appeal by stipulation filed in the district court, or the district court may dismiss the appeal on the appellant's motion, with notice to all parties. If a notice of appeal has been filed, but the case has not been placed on this Court's docket within the time prescribed for docketing, the district court may dismiss the appeal on the appellee's motion, with notice to all parties, and may make any just order with respect to costs. If the district court has denied the appellee's motion to dismiss the appeal, the appellee may move this Court to docket and dismiss the appeal by filing an original and 10 copies of a motion presented in conformity with Rules 21 and 33.2. The motion shall be accompanied by proof of service as required by Rule 29, and by a certificate from the clerk of the district court, certifying that a notice of appeal was filed and that the appellee's motion to dismiss was denied. The appellant may not

thereafter file a jurisdictional statement without special leave of the Court, and the Court may allow costs against the appellant.

6. Within 30 days after the case is placed on this Court's docket, the appellee may file a motion to dismiss, to affirm, or in the alternative to affirm or dismiss. Forty copies of the motion shall be filed, except that an appellee proceeding *in forma pauperis* under Rule 39, including an inmate of an institution, shall file the number of copies required for a petition by such a person under Rule 12.2, together with a motion for leave to proceed *in forma pauperis*, a copy of which shall precede and be attached to each copy of the motion to dismiss, to affirm, or in the alternative to affirm or dismiss. The motion shall follow, insofar as applicable, the form for a brief in opposition prescribed by Rule 15, and shall comply in all respects with Rule 21.

7. The Clerk will distribute the jurisdictional statement to the Court for its consideration upon receiving an express waiver of the right to file a motion to dismiss or to affirm or, if no waiver or motion is filed, upon the expiration of the time allowed for filing. If a motion to dismiss or to affirm is timely filed, the Clerk will distribute the jurisdictional statement, motion, and any brief opposing the motion to the Court for its consideration no less than 10 days after the motion is filed.

8. Any appellant may file a brief opposing a motion to dismiss or to affirm, but distribution and consideration by the Court under paragraph 7 of this Rule will not be deferred pending its receipt. Forty copies shall be filed, except that an appellant proceeding *in forma pauperis* under Rule 39, including an inmate of an institution, shall file the number of copies required for a petition by such a person under Rule 12.2. The brief shall be served as required by Rule 29.

9. If a cross-appeal has been docketed, distribution of both jurisdictional statements will be deferred until the cross-appeal is due for distribution under this Rule.

10. Any party may file a supplemental brief at any time while a jurisdictional statement is pending, calling attention to new

cases, new legislation, or other intervening matter not available at the time of the party's last filing. A supplemental brief shall be restricted to new matter and shall follow, insofar as applicable, the form for a brief in opposition prescribed by Rule 15. Forty copies shall be filed, except that a party proceeding *in forma pauperis* under Rule 39, including an inmate of an institution, shall file the number of copies required for a petition by such a person under Rule 12.2. The supplemental brief shall be served as required by Rule 29.

11. The clerk of the district court shall retain possession of the record until notified by the Clerk of this Court to certify and transmit it. See Rule 12.7.

12. After considering the documents distributed under this Rule, the Court may dispose summarily of the appeal on the merits, note probable jurisdiction, or postpone consideration of jurisdiction until a hearing of the case on the merits. If not disposed of summarily, the case stands for briefing and oral argument on the merits. If consideration of jurisdiction is postponed, counsel, at the outset of their briefs and at oral argument, shall address the question of jurisdiction. If the record has not previously been filed in this Court, the Clerk of this Court will request the clerk of the court in possession of the record to certify and transmit it.

13. If the Clerk determines that a jurisdictional statement submitted timely and in good faith is in a form that does not comply with this Rule or with Rule 33 or Rule 34, the Clerk will return it with a letter indicating the deficiency. If a corrected jurisdictional statement is received no more than 60 days after the date of the Clerk's letter, its filing will be deemed timely.

Rule 19. Procedure on a Certified Question

1. A United States court of appeals may certify to this Court a question or proposition of law on which it seeks instruction for the proper decision of a case. The certificate shall contain

a statement of the nature of the case and the facts on which the question or proposition of law arises. Only questions or propositions of law may be certified, and they shall be stated separately and with precision. The certificate shall be prepared as required by Rule 33.2 and shall be signed by the clerk of the court of appeals.

2. When a question is certified by a United States court of appeals, this Court, on its own motion or that of a party, may consider and decide the entire matter in controversy. See 28 U.S.C. § 1254(2).

3. When a question is certified, the Clerk will notify the parties and docket the case. Counsel shall then enter their appearances. After docketing, the Clerk will submit the certificate to the Court for a preliminary examination to determine whether the case should be briefed, set for argument, or dismissed. No brief may be filed until the preliminary examination of the certificate is completed.

4. If the Court orders the case briefed or set for argument, the parties will be notified and permitted to file briefs. The Clerk of this Court then will request the clerk of the court in possession of the record to certify and transmit it. Any portion of the record to which the parties wish to direct the Court's particular attention should be printed in a joint appendix, prepared in conformity with Rule 26 by the appellant or petitioner in the court of appeals, but the fact that any part of the record has not been printed does not prevent the parties or the Court from relying on it.

5. A brief on the merits in a case involving a certified question shall comply with Rules 24, 25, and 33.1, except that the brief for the party who is the appellant or petitioner below shall be filed within 45 days of the order requiring briefs or setting the case for argument.

Rule 20. Procedure on a Petition for an Extraordinary Writ

1. Issuance by the Court of an extraordinary writ authorized by 28 U.S.C. § 1651(a) is not a matter of right, but of discretion

sparingly exercised. To justify the granting of any such writ, the petition must show that the writ will be in aid of the Court's appellate jurisdiction, that exceptional circumstances warrant the exercise of the Court's discretionary powers, and that adequate relief cannot be obtained in any other form or from any other court.

2. A petition seeking a writ authorized by 28 U.S.C. § 1651(a), § 2241, or § 2254(a) shall be prepared in all respects as required by Rules 33 and 34. The petition shall be captioned "In re [name of petitioner]" and shall follow, insofar as applicable, the form of a petition for a writ of certiorari prescribed by Rule 14. All contentions in support of the petition shall be included in the petition. The case will be placed on the docket when 40 copies of the petition are filed with the Clerk and the docket fee is paid, except that a petitioner proceeding *in forma pauperis* under Rule 39, including an inmate of an institution, shall file the number of copies required for a petition by such a person under Rule 12.2, together with a motion for leave to proceed *in forma pauperis*, a copy of which shall precede and be attached to each copy of the petition. The petition shall be served as required by Rule 29 (subject to subparagraph 4(b) of this Rule).

3.   (a) A petition seeking a writ of prohibition, a writ of mandamus, or both in the alternative shall state the name and office or function of every person against whom relief is sought and shall set out with particularity why the relief sought is not available in any other court. A copy of the judgment with respect to which the writ is sought, including any related opinion, shall be appended to the petition together with any other document essential to understanding the petition.

   (b) The petition shall be served on every party to the proceeding with respect to which relief is sought. Within 30 days after the petition is placed on the docket, a party shall file 40 copies of any brief or briefs in opposition thereto, which shall comply fully with Rule 15. If a party named as a respondent does not wish to respond to the petition, that party may so advise the

Clerk and all other parties by letter. All persons served are deemed respondents for all purposes in the proceedings in this Court.

4.   (a) A petition seeking a writ of habeas corpus shall comply with the requirements of 28 U.S.C. §§ 2241 and 2242, and in particular with the provision in the last paragraph of § 2242, which requires a statement of the "reasons for not making application to the district court of the district in which the applicant is held." If the relief sought is from the judgment of a state court, the petition shall set out specifically how and where the petitioner has exhausted available remedies in the state courts or otherwise comes within the provisions of 28 U.S.C. § 2254(b). To justify the granting of a writ of habeas corpus, the petitioner must show that exceptional circumstances warrant the exercise of the Court's discretionary powers, and that adequate relief cannot be obtained in any other form or from any other court. This writ is rarely granted.

    (b) Habeas corpus proceedings are *ex parte*, unless the Court requires the respondent to show cause why the petition for a writ of habeas corpus should not be granted. A response, if ordered, shall comply fully with Rule 15. Neither the denial of the petition, without more, nor an order of transfer to a district court under the authority of 28 U.S.C. § 2241(b), is an adjudication on the merits, and therefore does not preclude further application to another court for the relief sought.

5. The Clerk will distribute the documents to the Court for its consideration when a brief in opposition under subparagraph 3(b) of this Rule has been filed, when a response under subparagraph 4(b) has been ordered and filed, when the time to file has expired, or when the right to file has been expressly waived.

6. If the Court orders the case set for argument, the Clerk will notify the parties whether additional briefs are required, when they shall be filed, and, if the case involves a petition for a

common-law writ of certiorari, that the parties shall prepare a joint appendix in accordance with Rule 26.

Part V. Motions and Applications
Rule 21. Motions to the Court

1. Every motion to the Court shall clearly state its purpose and the facts on which it is based and may present legal argument in support thereof. No separate brief may be filed. A motion should be concise and shall comply with any applicable page limits. Rule 22 governs an application addressed to a single Justice.

2.   (a) A motion in any action within the Court's original jurisdiction shall comply with Rule 17.3.

  (b) A motion to dismiss as moot (or a suggestion of mootness), a motion for leave to file a brief as *amicus curiae*, and any motion the granting of which would dispose of the entire case or would affect the final judgment to be entered (other than a motion to docket and dismiss under Rule 18.5 or a motion for voluntary dismissal under Rule 46) shall be prepared as required by Rule 33.1, and 40 copies shall be filed, except that a movant proceeding *in forma pauperis* under Rule 39, including an inmate of an institution, shall file a motion prepared as required by Rule 33.2, and shall file the number of copies required for a petition by such a person under Rule 12.2. The motion shall be served as required by Rule 29.

  (c) Any other motion to the Court shall be prepared as required by Rule 33.2; the moving party shall file an original and 10 copies. The Court subsequently may order the moving party to prepare the motion as required by Rule 33.1; in that event, the party shall file 40 copies.

3. A motion to the Court shall be filed with the Clerk and shall be accompanied by proof of service as required by Rule 29. No motion may be presented in open Court, other than a motion for admission to the Bar, except when the proceeding

to which it refers is being argued. Oral argument on a motion will not be permitted unless the Court so directs.

4. Any response to a motion shall be filed as promptly as possible considering the nature of the relief sought and any asserted need for emergency action, and, in any event, within 10 days of receipt, unless the Court or a Justice, or the Clerk under Rule 30.4, orders otherwise. A response to a motion prepared as required by Rule 33.1 shall be prepared in the same manner if time permits. In an appropriate case, the Court may act on a motion without waiting for a response.

Rule 22. Applications to Individual Justices

1. An application addressed to an individual Justice shall be filed with the Clerk, who will transmit it promptly to the Justice concerned if an individual Justice has authority to grant the sought relief.

2. The original and two copies of any application addressed to an individual Justice shall be prepared as required by Rule 33.2, and shall be accompanied by proof of service as required by Rule 29.

3. An application shall be addressed to the Justice allotted to the Circuit from which the case arises. When the Circuit Justice is unavailable for any reason, the application addressed to that Justice will be distributed to the Justice then available who is next junior to the Circuit Justice; the turn of the Chief Justice follows that of the most junior Justice.

4. A Justice denying an application will note the denial thereon. Thereafter, unless action thereon is restricted by law to the Circuit Justice or is untimely under Rule 30.2, the party making an application, except in the case of an application for an extension of time, may renew it to any other Justice, subject to the provisions of this Rule. Except when the denial is without prejudice, a renewed application is not favored. Renewed application is made by a letter to the Clerk, designating the Justice to whom the application is to be directed, and accompanied by 10 copies of the original application and proof of service as required by Rule 29.

5. A Justice to whom an application for a stay or for bail is submitted may refer it to the Court for determination.
6. The Clerk will advise all parties concerned, by appropriately speedy means, of the disposition made of an application.

Rule 23. Stays

1. A stay may be granted by a Justice as permitted by law.
2. A party to a judgment sought to be reviewed may present to a Justice an application to stay the enforcement of that judgment. See 28 U.S.C. § 2101(f).
3. An application for a stay shall set out with particularity why the relief sought is not available from any other court or judge. Except in the most extraordinary circumstances, an application for a stay will not be entertained unless the relief requested was first sought in the appropriate court or courts below or from a judge or judges thereof. An application for a stay shall identify the judgment sought to be reviewed and have appended thereto a copy of the order and opinion, if any, and a copy of the order, if any, of the court or judge below denying the relief sought, and shall set out specific reasons why a stay is justified. The form and content of an application for a stay are governed by Rules 22 and 33.2.
4. A judge, court, or Justice granting an application for a stay pending review by this Court may condition the stay on the filing of a supersedeas bond having an approved surety or sureties. The bond will be conditioned on the satisfaction of the judgment in full, together with any costs, interest, and damages for delay that may be awarded. If a part of the judgment sought to be reviewed has already been satisfied, or is otherwise secured, the bond may be conditioned on the satisfaction of the part of the judgment not otherwise secured or satisfied, together with costs, interest, and damages.

Part VI. Briefs on the Merits and Oral Argument
Rule 24. Briefs on the Merits: In General

1. A brief on the merits for a petitioner or an appellant shall comply in all respects with Rules 33.1 and 34 and shall contain in the order here indicated:

   (a) The questions presented for review under Rule 14.1(a). The questions shall be set out on the first page following the cover, and no other information may appear on that page. The phrasing of the questions presented need not be identical with that in the petition for a writ of certiorari or the jurisdictional statement, but the brief may not raise additional questions or change the substance of the questions already presented in those documents. At its option, however, the Court may consider a plain error not among the questions presented but evident from the record and otherwise within its jurisdiction to decide.

   (b) A list of all parties to the proceeding in the court whose judgment is under review (unless the caption of the case in this Court contains the names of all parties). Any amended list of parent companies and non-wholly owned subsidiaries as required by Rule 29.6 shall be placed here.

   (c) If the brief exceeds five pages, a table of contents and a table of cited authorities.

   (d) Citations of the official and unofficial reports of the opinions and orders entered in the case by courts and administrative agencies.

   (e) A concise statement of the basis for jurisdiction in this Court, including the statutory provisions and time factors on which jurisdiction rests.

   (f) The constitutional provisions, treaties, statutes, ordinances, and regulations involved in the case, set out verbatim with appropriate citation. If the provisions involved are lengthy, their citation alone suffices at this point, and their pertinent text, if not already set out in the petition for a writ of certiorari, jurisdictional statement, or an appendix to either document, shall be set out in an appendix to the brief.

(g) A concise statement of the case, setting out the facts material to the consideration of the questions presented, with appropriate references to the joint appendix, e.g., App. 12, or to the record, e.g., Record 12.

(h) A summary of the argument, suitably paragraphed. The summary should be a clear and concise condensation of the argument made in the body of the brief; mere repetition of the headings under which the argument is arranged is not sufficient.

(i) The argument, exhibiting clearly the points of fact and of law presented and citing the authorities and statutes relied on.

(j) A conclusion specifying with particularity the relief the party seeks.

2. A brief on the merits for a respondent or an appellee shall conform to the foregoing requirements, except that items required by subparagraphs 1(a), (b), (d), (e), (f), and (g) of this Rule need not be included unless the respondent or appellee is dissatisfied with their presentation by the opposing party.

3. A brief on the merits may not exceed the page limitations specified in Rule 33.1(g). An appendix to a brief may include only relevant material, and counsel are cautioned not to include in an appendix arguments or citations that properly belong in the body of the brief.

4. A reply brief shall conform to those portions of this Rule applicable to the brief for a respondent or an appellee, but, if appropriately divided by topical headings, need not contain a summary of the argument.

5. A reference to the joint appendix or to the record set out in any brief shall indicate the appropriate page number. If the reference is to an exhibit, the page numbers at which the exhibit appears, at which it was offered in evidence, and at which it was ruled on by the judge shall be indicated, e.g., Pl. Exh. 14, Record 199, 2134.

6. A brief shall be concise, logically arranged with proper headings, and free of irrelevant, immaterial, or scandalous matter.

The Court may disregard or strike a brief that does not comply with this paragraph.

Rule 25. Briefs on the Merits: Number of Copies and Time to File

1. The petitioner or appellant shall file 40 copies of the brief on the merits within 45 days of the order granting the writ of certiorari, noting probable jurisdiction, or postponing consideration of jurisdiction.
2. The respondent or appellee shall file 40 copies of the brief on the merits within 30 days after receiving the brief for the petitioner or appellant.
3. The petitioner or appellant shall file 40 copies of the reply brief, if any, within 30 days after receiving the brief for the respondent or appellee, but any reply brief must actually be received by the Clerk no more than one week before the date of oral argument.
4. The time periods stated in paragraphs 1 and 2 of this Rule may be extended as provided in Rule 30. An application to extend the time to file a brief on the merits is not favored. If a case is advanced for hearing, the time to file briefs on the merits may be abridged as circumstances require pursuant to an order of the Court on its own motion or that of a party.
5. A party wishing to present late authorities, newly enacted legislation, or other intervening matter that was not available in time to be included in a brief may file 40 copies of a supplemental brief, restricted to such new matter and otherwise presented in conformity with these Rules, up to the time the case is called for oral argument or by leave of the Court thereafter.
6. After a case has been argued or submitted, the Clerk will not file any brief, except that of a party filed by leave of the Court.
7. The Clerk will not file any brief that is not accompanied by proof of service as required by Rule 29.

Rule 26. Joint Appendix

1. Unless the Clerk has allowed the parties to use the deferred method described in paragraph 4 of this Rule, the petitioner or appellant, within 45 days after entry of the order granting the writ of certiorari, noting probable jurisdiction, or postponing consideration of jurisdiction, shall file 40 copies of a joint appendix, prepared as required by Rule 33.1. The joint appendix shall contain: (1) the relevant docket entries in all the courts below; (2) any relevant pleadings, jury instructions, findings, conclusions, or opinions; (3) the judgment, order, or decision under review; and (4) any other parts of the record that the parties particularly wish to bring to the Court's attention. Any of the foregoing items already reproduced in a petition for a writ of certiorari, jurisdictional statement, brief in opposition to a petition for a writ of certiorari, motion to dismiss or affirm, or any appendix to the foregoing, that was prepared as required by Rule 33.1, need not be reproduced again in the joint appendix. The petitioner or appellant shall serve three copies of the joint appendix on each of the other parties to the proceeding as required by Rule 29.

2. The parties are encouraged to agree on the contents of the joint appendix. In the absence of agreement, the petitioner or appellant, within 10 days after entry of the order granting the writ of certiorari, noting probable jurisdiction, or postponing consideration of jurisdiction, shall serve on the respondent or appellee a designation of parts of the record to be included in the joint appendix. Within 10 days after receiving the designation, a respondent or appellee who considers the parts of the record so designated insufficient shall serve on the petitioner or appellant a designation of additional parts to be included in the joint appendix, and the petitioner or appellant shall include the parts so designated. If the Court has permitted the respondent or appellee to proceed *in forma pauperis*, the petitioner or appellant may seek by motion to be excused from printing portions of the record the petitioner or appel-
   .. considers unnecessary. In making these designations,
   nsel should include only those materials the Court should

examine; unnecessary designations should be avoided. The record is on file with the Clerk and available to the Justices, and counsel may refer in briefs and in oral argument to relevant portions of the record not included in the joint appendix.

3. When the joint appendix is filed, the petitioner or appellant immediately shall file with the Clerk a statement of the cost of printing 50 copies and shall serve a copy of the statement on each of the other parties as required by Rule 29. Unless the parties agree otherwise, the cost of producing the joint appendix shall be paid initially by the petitioner or appellant; but a petitioner or appellant who considers that parts of the record designated by the respondent or appellee are unnecessary for the determination of the issues presented may so advise the respondent or appellee, who then shall advance the cost of printing the additional parts, unless the Court or a Justice otherwise fixes the initial allocation of the costs. The cost of printing the joint appendix is taxed as a cost in the case, but if a party unnecessarily causes matter to be included in the joint appendix or prints excessive copies, the Court may impose these costs on that party.

4. (a) On the parties' request, the Clerk may allow preparation of the joint appendix to be deferred until after the briefs have been filed. In that event, the petitioner or appellant shall file the joint appendix no more than 14 days after receiving the brief for the respondent or appellee. The provisions of paragraphs 1, 2, and 3 of this Rule shall be followed, except that the designations referred to therein shall be made by each party when that party's brief is served. Deferral of the joint appendix is not favored.

    (b) If the deferred method is used, the briefs on the merits may refer to the pages of the record. In that event, the joint appendix shall include in brackets on each page thereof the page number of the record where that material may be found. A party wishing to refer directly to the pages of the joint appendix may serve and file copies of its brief prepared as required by Rule 33.2

within the time provided by Rule 25, with appropriate references to the pages of the record. In that event, within 10 days after the joint appendix is filed, copies of the brief prepared as required by Rule 33.1 containing references to the pages of the joint appendix in place of, or in addition to, the initial references to the pages of the record, shall be served and filed. No other change may be made in the brief as initially served and filed, except that typographical errors may be corrected.

5. The joint appendix shall be prefaced by a table of contents showing the parts of the record that it contains, in the order in which the parts are set out, with references to the pages of the joint appendix at which each part begins. The relevant docket entries shall be set out after the table of contents, followed by the other parts of the record in chronological order. When testimony contained in the reporter's transcript of proceedings is set out in the joint appendix, the page of the transcript at which the testimony appears shall be indicated in brackets immediately before the statement that is set out. Omissions in the transcript or in any other document printed in the joint appendix shall be indicated by asterisks. Immaterial formal matters (e.g., captions, subscriptions, acknowledgments) shall be omitted. A question and its answer may be contained in a single paragraph.

6. Exhibits designated for inclusion in the joint appendix may be contained in a separate volume or volumes suitably indexed. The transcript of a proceeding before an administrative agency, board, commission, or officer used in an action in a district court or court of appeals is regarded as an exhibit for the purposes of this paragraph.

7. The Court, on its own motion or that of a party, may dispense with the requirement of a joint appendix and may permit a case to be heard on the original record (with such copies of the record, or relevant parts thereof, as the Court may require) or on the appendix used in the court below, if it conforms to the requirements of this Rule.

8. For good cause, the time limits specified in this Rule may be

shortened or extended by the Court or a Justice, or by the Clerk under Rule 30.4.

Rule 27. The Calendar

1. From time to time, the Clerk will prepare a calendar of cases ready for argument. A case ordinarily will not be called for argument less than two weeks after the brief on the merits for the respondent or appellee is due.
2. The Clerk will advise counsel when they are required to appear for oral argument and will publish a hearing list in advance of each argument session for the convenience of counsel and the information of the public.
3. The Court, on its own motion or that of a party, may order that two or more cases involving the same or related questions be argued together as one case or on such other terms as the Court may prescribe.

Rule 28. Oral Argument

1. Oral argument should emphasize and clarify the written arguments in the briefs on the merits. Counsel should assume that all Justices have read the briefs before oral argument. Oral argument read from a prepared text is not favored.
2. The petitioner or appellant shall open and may conclude the argument. A cross writ of certiorari or cross-appeal will be argued with the initial writ of certiorari or appeal as one case in the time allowed for that one case, and the Court will advise the parties who shall open and close.
3. Unless the Court directs otherwise, each side is allowed one-half hour for argument. Counsel is not required to use all the allotted time. Any request for additional time to argue shall be presented by motion under Rule 21 no more than 15 days after the petitioner's or appellant's brief on the merits is filed, and shall set out specifically and concisely why the case cannot be presented within the half hour limitation. Additional time is rarely accorded.

4. Only one attorney will be heard for each side, except by leave of the Court on motion filed no more than 15 days after the respondent's or appellee's brief on the merits is filed. Any request for divided argument shall be presented by motion under Rule 21 and shall set out specifically and concisely why more than one attorney should be allowed to argue. Divided argument is not favored.

5. Regardless of the number of counsel participating in oral argument, counsel making the opening argument shall present the case fairly and completely and not reserve points of substance for rebuttal.

6. Oral argument will not be allowed on behalf of any party for whom a brief has not been filed.

7. By leave of the Court, and subject to paragraph 4 of this Rule, counsel for an *amicus curiae* whose brief has been filed as provided in Rule 37 may argue orally on the side of a party, with the consent of that party. In the absence of consent, counsel for an *amicus curiae* may seek leave of the Court to argue orally by a motion setting out specifically and concisely why oral argument would provide assistance to the Court not otherwise available. Such a motion will be granted only in the most extraordinary circumstances.

Part VII. Practice and Procedure
Rule 29. Filing and Service of Documents; Special Notifications; Corporate Listing

1. Any document required or permitted to be presented to the Court or to a Justice shall be filed with the Clerk.

2. A document is timely filed if it is sent to the Clerk through the United States Postal Service by first-class mail (including express or priority mail), postage prepaid, and bears a postmark showing that the document was mailed on or before the last day for filing. Commercial postage meter labels alone are not acceptable. If submitted by an inmate confined in an institution, a document is timely filed if it is deposited in the

institution's internal mail system on or before the last day for filing and is accompanied by a notarized statement or declaration in compliance with 28 U.S.C. § 1746 setting out the date of deposit and stating that first-class postage has been prepaid. If the postmark is missing or not legible, the Clerk will require the person who mailed the document to submit a notarized statement or declaration in compliance with 28 U.S.C. § 1746 setting out the details of the mailing and stating that the mailing took place on a particular date within the permitted time. A document also is timely filed if it is forwarded through a private delivery or courier service and is actually received by the Clerk within the time permitted for filing.

3. Any document required by these Rules to be served may be served personally or by mail on each party to the proceeding at or before the time of filing. If the document has been prepared as required by Rule 33.1, three copies shall be served on each other party separately represented in the proceeding. If the document has been prepared as required by Rule 33.2, service of a single copy on each other separately represented party suffices. If personal service is made, it shall consist of delivery at the office of the counsel of record, either to counsel or to an employee therein. If service is by mail, it shall consist of depositing the document with the United States Postal Service, with no less than first-class postage prepaid, addressed to counsel of record at the proper post office address. When a party is not represented by counsel, service shall be made on the party, personally or by mail.

4.   (a) If the United States or any federal department, office, agency, officer, or employee is a party to be served, service shall be made on the Solicitor General of the United States, Room 5614, Department of Justice, 10th St. and Constitution Ave., N.W., Washington, D.C. 20530. When an agency of the United States that is a party is authorized by law to appear before this Court on its own behalf, or when an officer or employee of the United States is a party, the agency,

officer, or employee shall be served in addition to the Solicitor General.

(b) In any proceeding in this Court in which the constitutionality of an Act of Congress is drawn into question, and neither the United States nor any federal department, office, agency, officer, or employee is a party, the initial document filed in this Court shall recite that 28 U.S.C. § 2403(a) may apply and shall be served on the Solicitor General of the United States, Room 5614, Department of Justice, 10th St. and Constitution Ave., N.W., Washington, D.C. 20530. In such a proceeding from any court of the United States, as defined by 28 U.S.C. § 451, the initial document also shall state whether that court, pursuant to 28 U.S.C. § 2403(a), certified to the Attorney General the fact that the constitutionality of an Act of Congress was drawn into question. See Rule 14.1(e)(v).

(c) In any proceeding in this Court in which the constitutionality of any statute of a State is drawn into question, and neither the State nor any agency, officer, or employee thereof is a party, the initial document filed in this Court shall recite that 28 U.S.C. § 2403(b) may apply and shall be served on the Attorney General of that State. In such a proceeding from any court of the United States, as defined by 28 U.S.C. § 451, the initial document also shall state whether that court, pursuant to 28 U.S.C. § 2403(b), certified to the State Attorney General the fact that the constitutionality of a statute of that State was drawn into question. See Rule 14.1(e)(v).

5. Proof of service, when required by these Rules, shall accompany the document when it is presented to the Clerk for filing and shall be separate from it. Proof of service shall contain, or be accompanied by, a statement that all parties required to be served have been served, together with a list of the names, addresses, and telephone numbers of counsel indicating the name of the party or parties each counsel repre-

sents. It is not necessary that service on each party required to be served be made in the same manner or evidenced by the same proof. Proof of service may consist of any one of the following:

(a) an acknowledgment of service, signed by counsel of record for the party served;

(b) a certificate of service, reciting the facts and circumstances of service in compliance with the appropriate paragraph or paragraphs of this Rule, and signed by a member of the Bar of this Court representing the party on whose behalf service is made or by an attorney appointed to represent that party under the Criminal Justice Act of 1964, see 18 U.S.C. § 3006A(d)(6), or under any other applicable federal statute; or

(c) a notarized affidavit or declaration in compliance with 28 U.S.C. § 1746, reciting the facts and circumstances of service in accordance with the appropriate paragraph or paragraphs of this Rule, whenever service is made by any person not a member of the Bar of this Court and not an attorney appointed to represent a party under the Criminal Justice Act of 1964, see 18 U.S.C. § 3006A(d)(6), or under any other applicable federal statute.

6. Every document, except a joint appendix or *amicus curiae* brief, filed by or on behalf of one or more corporations shall list all parent companies and nonwholly owned subsidiaries of each of the corporate filers. If there is no parent or subsidiary company to be listed, a notation to this effect shall be included in the document. If a list has been included in a document filed earlier in the case, reference may be made to the earlier document (except when the earlier list appeared in an application for an extension of time or for a stay), and only amendments to the list to make it current need be included in the document being filed.

Rule 30. Computation and Extension of Time

1. In the computation of any period of time prescribed or allowed by these Rules, by order of the Court, or by an appli-

cable statute, the day of the act, event, or default from which the designated period begins to run is not included. The last day of the period shall be included, unless it is a Saturday, Sunday, federal legal holiday listed in 5 U.S.C. § 6103, or day on which the Court building is closed by order of the Court or the Chief Justice, in which event the period shall extend until the end of the next day that is not a Saturday, Sunday, federal legal holiday, or day on which the Court building is closed.

2. Whenever a Justice or the Clerk is empowered by law or these Rules to extend the time to file any document, an application seeking an extension shall be filed within the period sought to be extended. An application to extend the time to file a petition for a writ of certiorari or to file a jurisdictional statement must be received by the Clerk at least 10 days before the specified final filing date as computed under these Rules; if received less than 10 days before the final filing date, such application will not be granted except in the most extraordinary circumstances.

3. An application to extend the time to file a petition for a writ of certiorari, to file a jurisdictional statement, to file a reply brief on the merits, or to file a petition for rehearing shall be made to an individual Justice and presented and served on all other parties as provided by Rule 22. Once denied, such an application may not be renewed.

4. An application to extend the time to file any document or paper other than those specified in paragraph 3 of this Rule may be presented in the form of a letter to the Clerk setting out specific reasons why an extension of time is justified. The letter shall be served on all other parties as required by Rule 29. The application may be acted on by the Clerk in the first instance, and any party aggrieved by the Clerk's action may request that the application be submitted to a Justice or to the Court. The Clerk will report action under this paragraph to the Court as instructed.

Rule 31. Translations

Whenever any record to be transmitted to this Court contains material written in a foreign language without a translation made under the authority of the lower court, or admitted to be correct, the clerk of the court transmitting the record shall advise the Clerk of this Court immediately so that this Court may order that a translation be supplied and, if necessary, printed as part of the joint appendix.

Rule 32. Models, Diagrams, and Exhibits

1. Models, diagrams, and exhibits of material forming part of the evidence taken in a case and brought to this Court for its inspection shall be placed in the custody of the Clerk at least two weeks before the case is to be heard or submitted.
2. All models, diagrams, and exhibits of material placed in the custody of the Clerk shall be removed by the parties no more than 40 days after the case is decided. If this is not done, the Clerk will notify counsel to remove the articles forthwith. If they are not removed within a reasonable time thereafter, the Clerk will destroy them or dispose of them in any other appropriate way.

Rule 33. Document Preparation: Booklet Format; 8½- by 11-Inch Paper Format

1. Booklet Format: (a) Except for a document expressly permitted by these Rules to be submitted on 8½- by 11-inch paper, see, e.g., Rules 21, 22, and 39, every document filed with the Court shall be prepared using typesetting (e.g., word-processing, electronic publishing, or image setting) and reproduced by offset printing, photocopying, or similar process. The process used must produce a clear, black image on white paper.

    (b) The text of every document, including any appendix thereto, except a document permitted to be produced on 8½- by 11-inch paper, shall be typeset in standard 11-point or larger type with 2-point or more leading between lines. The type size and face shall be no smaller than that contained in the *United States Reports* beginning with Volume 453. Type size and face shall be consistent throughout. No attempt should be made to reduce, compress, or condense the typeface in a manner that would increase the content of a document. Quotations in excess of three lines shall be indented. Footnotes shall appear in print as standard 9-point or larger type with 2-point or more leading between lines. The text of the document must appear on both sides of the page.

(c) Every document, except one permitted to be produced on 8½- by 11-inch paper, shall be produced on paper that is opaque, unglazed, 6⅛ by 9¼ inches in size, and not less than 60 pounds in weight, and shall have margins of at least three fourths of an inch on all sides. The text field, including footnotes, should be approximately 4⅛ by 7⅛ inches. The document shall be bound firmly in at least two places along the left margin (saddle stitch or perfect binding preferred) so as to permit easy opening, and no part of the text should be obscured by the binding. Spiral, plastic, metal, and string bindings may not be used. Copies of patent documents, except opinions, may be duplicated in such size as is necessary in a separate appendix.

(d) Every document, except one permitted to be produced on 8½- by 11-inch paper, shall comply with the page limits shown on the chart in subparagraph 1(g) of this Rule. The page limits do not include the pages containing the questions presented, the list of parties and corporate affiliates of the filing party, the table of contents, the table of cited authorities, or any appendix. Verbatim quotations required under Rule 14.1(f), if set out in the text of a brief rather than in the appendix, are also excluded. For good cause, the Court or a Justice may grant leave to file a document in excess of the page limits, but application for such leave is not favored. An application to exceed page limits shall comply with Rule 22 and must be received by the Clerk at least 15 days before the filing date of the document in question, except in the most extraordinary circumstances.

(e) Every document, except one permitted to be produced on 8½- by 11-inch paper, shall have a suitable cover consisting of 65-pound weight paper in the color indicated on the chart in subparagraph 1(g) of this Rule. If a separate appendix to any document is filed, the color of its cover shall be the same as that of the cover of the document it supports. The Clerk will furnish a color chart upon request. Counsel shall ensure that there is adequate contrast between the printing and the color of the cover. A document filed by the United States, or by any other federal party represented by the Solicitor General, shall have a gray cover. A joint appendix, answer to a bill of complaint, motion for leave to intervene, and any other document not listed in subparagraph 1(g) of this Rule shall have a tan cover.

(f) Forty copies of a document prepared under this paragraph shall be filed.

(g) Page limits and cover colors for booklet-format documents are as follows:

Type of Document	Page Limits	Color of Cover
i. Petition for a Writ of Certiorari (Rule 14); Motion for Leave to file a Bill of Complaint and Brief in Support (Rule 17.3); Jurisdictional Statement (Rule 18.3); Petition for an Extraordinary Writ (Rule 20.2)	30	white

Type of Document	Page Limits	Color of Cover
ii. Brief in Opposition (Rule 15.3); Brief in Opposition to Motion for Leave to file an Original Action (Rule 17.5); Motion to Dismiss or Affirm (Rule 18.6); Brief in Opposition to Mandamus or Prohibition (Rule 20.3 (b)); Response to a Petition for Habeas Corpus (Rule 20.4)	30	orange
iii. Reply to Brief in Opposition (Rules 15.6 and 17.5); Brief Opposing a Motion to Dismiss or Affirm (Rule 18.8)	10	tan
iv. Supplemental Brief (Rules 15.8, 17, 18.10, and 25.5)	10	tan
v. Brief on the Merits by Petitioner or Appellant (Rule 24); Exceptions by Plaintiff to Report of Special Master (Rule 17)	50	light blue
vi. Brief on the Merits by Respondent or Appellee (Rule 24.2); Brief on the Merits for Respondent or Appellee Supporting Petitioner or Appellant (Rule 12.6); Exceptions by Party Other than Plaintiff to Report of Special Master (Rule 17)	50	light red

Type of Document	Page Limits	Color of Cover
vii. Reply Brief on the Merits (Rule 24.4)	20	yellow
viii. Reply to Plaintiff's Exceptions to Report of Special Master (Rule 17)	50	orange
ix. Reply to Exceptions by Party Other Than Plaintiff to Report of Special Master (Rule 17)	50	yellow
x. Brief for an *Amicus Curiae* at the Petition Stage (Rule 37.2)	20	cream
xi. Brief for an *Amicus Curiae* in Support of the Plaintiff, Petitioner, or Appellant, or in Support of Neither Party, on the Merits, or in an Original Action at the Exceptions Stage (Rule 37.3)	30	light green
xii. Brief for an *Amicus Curiae* in Support of the Defendant, Respondent, or Appellee, on the Merits or in an Original Action at the Exceptions Stage (Rule 37.3)	30	dark green
xiii. Petition for Rehearing (Rule 44)	10	tan

parties may be of considerable help to the Court. An *amicus curiae* brief that does not serve this purpose burdens the Court, and its filing is not favored.

2.   (a) An *amicus curiae* brief submitted before the Court's consideration of a petition for a writ of certiorari, motion for leave to file a bill of complaint, jurisdictional statement, or petition for an extraordinary writ may be filed if accompanied by the written consent of all parties, or if the Court grants leave to file under subparagraph 2(b) of this Rule. The brief shall be submitted within the time allowed for filing a brief in opposition or for filing a motion to dismiss or affirm. The *amicus curiae* brief shall specify whether consent was granted, and its cover shall identify the party supported.

   (b) When a party to the case has withheld consent, a motion for leave to file an *amicus curiae* brief before the Court's consideration of a petition for a writ of certiorari, motion for leave to file a bill of complaint, jurisdictional statement, or petition for an extraordinary writ may be presented to the Court. The motion, prepared as required by Rule 33.1 and as one document with the brief sought to be filed, shall be submitted within the time allowed for filing an *amicus curiae* brief, and shall indicate the party or parties who have withheld consent and state the nature of the movant's interest. Such a motion is not favored.

3.   (a) An *amicus curiae* brief in a case before the Court for oral argument may be filed if accompanied by the written consent of all parties, or if the Court grants leave to file under subparagraph 3(b) of this Rule. The brief shall be submitted within the time allowed for filing the brief for the party supported, or if in support of neither party, within the time allowed for filing the petitioner's or appellant's brief. The *amicus curiae* brief shall specify whether consent was granted, and its cover shall identify the party supported or indicate whether it suggests affirmance or reversal. The Clerk

will not file a reply brief for an *amicus curiae*, or a brief for an *amicus curiae* in support of, or in opposition to, a petition for rehearing.

(b) When a party to a case before the Court for oral argument has withheld consent, a motion for leave to file an *amicus curiae* brief may be presented to the Court. The motion, prepared as required by Rule 33.1 and as one document with the brief sought to be filed, shall be submitted within the time allowed for filing an *amicus curiae* brief, and shall indicate the party or parties who have withheld consent and state the nature of the movant's interest.

4. No motion for leave to file an *amicus curiae* brief is necessary if the brief is presented on behalf of the United States by the Solicitor General; on behalf of any agency of the United States allowed by law to appear before this Court when submitted by the agency's authorized legal representative; on behalf of a State, Commonwealth, Territory, or Possession when submitted by its Attorney General; or on behalf of a city, county, town, or similar entity when submitted by its authorized law officer.

5. A brief or motion filed under this Rule shall be accompanied by proof of service as required by Rule 29, and shall comply with the applicable provisions of Rules 21, 24, and 33.1 (except that it suffices to set out in the brief the interest of the *amicus curiae*, the summary of the argument, the argument, and the conclusion). A motion for leave to file may not exceed five pages. A party served with the motion may file an objection thereto, stating concisely the reasons for withholding consent; the objection shall be prepared as required by Rule 33.2.

Rule 38. Fees

Under 28 U.S.C. § 1911, the fees charged by the Clerk are:

(a) for docketing a case on a petition for a writ of certiorari or on appeal or for docketing any other proceeding, except a certified question or a motion to docket and dismiss an appeal under Rule 18.5, $300;

(b) for filing a petition for rehearing or a motion for leave to file a petition for rehearing, $200;

(c) for reproducing and certifying any record or paper, $1 per page; and for comparing with the original thereof any photographic reproduction of any record or paper, when furnished by the person requesting its certification, $.50 per page;

(d) for a certificate bearing the seal of the Court, $10; and

(e) for a check paid to the Court, Clerk, or Marshal that is returned for lack of funds, $35.

Rule 39. Proceedings *In Forma Pauperis*

1. A party seeking to proceed *in forma pauperis* shall file a motion for leave to do so, together with the party's notarized affidavit or declaration (in compliance with 28 U.S.C. § 1746) in the form prescribed by the Federal Rules of Appellate Procedure, Form 4. See 28 U.S.C. § 1915. The motion shall state whether leave to proceed *in forma pauperis* was sought in any other court and, if so, whether leave was granted. If the United States district court or the United States court of appeals has appointed counsel under the Criminal Justice Act, see 18 U.S.C. § 3006A, or under any other applicable federal statute, no affidavit or declaration is required, but the motion shall cite the statute under which counsel was appointed.

2. If leave to proceed *in forma pauperis* is sought for the purpose of filing a document, the motion, and affidavit or declaration if required, shall be filed with that document and shall comply in every respect with Rule 21. As provided in that rule, it suffices to file an original and 10 copies, unless the party is an inmate confined in an institution and is not represented by counsel, in which case the original, alone, suffices. A copy of the motion shall precede and be attached to each copy of the accompanying document.

3. Except when these Rules expressly provide that a document shall be prepared as required by Rule 33.1, every document

presented by a party proceeding under this Rule shall be prepared as required by Rule 33.2 (unless such preparation is impossible). Every document shall be legible. While making due allowance for any case presented under this Rule by a person appearing pro se, the Clerk will not file any document if it does not comply with the substance of these Rules or is jurisdictionally out of time.

4. When the documents required by paragraphs 1 and 2 of this Rule are presented to the Clerk, accompanied by proof of service as required by Rule 29, they will be placed on the docket without the payment of a docket fee or any other fee.

5. The respondent or appellee in a case filed *in forma pauperis* shall respond in the same manner and within the same time as in any other case of the same nature, except that the filing of an original and 10 copies of a response prepared as required by Rule 33.2, with proof of service as required by Rule 29, suffices. The respondent or appellee may challenge the grounds for the motion for leave to proceed *in forma pauperis* in a separate document or in the response itself.

6. Whenever the Court appoints counsel for an indigent party in a case set for oral argument, the briefs on the merits submitted by that counsel, unless otherwise requested, shall be prepared under the Clerk's supervision. The Clerk also will reimburse appointed counsel for any necessary travel expenses to Washington, D.C., and return in connection with the argument.

7. In a case in which certiorari has been granted, probable jurisdiction noted, or consideration of jurisdiction postponed, this Court may appoint counsel to represent a party financially unable to afford an attorney to the extent authorized by the Criminal Justice Act of 1964, 18 U.S.C. § 3006A, or by any other applicable federal statute.

8. If satisfied that a petition for a writ of certiorari, jurisdictional statement, or petition for an extraordinary writ is frivolous or malicious, the Court may deny leave to proceed *in forma pauperis*.

Rule 40. Veterans, Seamen, and Military Cases

1. A veteran suing to establish reemployment rights under 38 U.S.C. § 2022, or under any other provision of law exempting veterans from the payment of fees or court costs, may file a motion for leave to proceed on papers prepared as required by Rule 33.2. The motion shall ask leave to proceed as a veteran and be accompanied by an affidavit or declaration setting out the moving party's veteran status. A copy of the motion shall precede and be attached to each copy of the petition for a writ of certiorari or other substantive document filed by the veteran.

2. A seaman suing under 28 U.S.C. § 1916 may proceed without prepayment of fees or costs or furnishing security therefor, but is not entitled to proceed under Rule 33.2, except as authorized by the Court on separate motion under Rule 39.

3. An accused person petitioning for a writ of certiorari to review a decision of the United States Court of Appeals for the Armed Forces under 28 U.S.C. § 1259 may proceed without prepayment of fees or costs or furnishing security therefor and without filing an affidavit of indigency, but is not entitled to proceed on papers prepared as required by Rule 33.2, except as authorized by the Court on separate motion under Rule 39.

Part VIII. Disposition of Cases
Rule 41. Opinions of the Court

Opinions of the Court will be released by the Clerk immediately upon their announcement from the bench, or as the Court otherwise directs. Thereafter, the Clerk will cause the opinions to be issued in slip form, and the Reporter of Decisions will prepare them for publication in the preliminary prints and bound volumes of the United States Reports.

Rule 42. Interest and Damages

1. If a judgment for money in a civil case is affirmed, any interest allowed by law is payable from the date the judgment un-

der review was entered. If a judgment is modified or reversed with a direction that a judgment for money be entered below, the mandate will contain instructions with respect to the allowance of interest. Interest in cases arising in a state court is allowed at the same rate that similar judgments bear interest in the courts of the State in which judgment is directed to be entered. Interest in cases arising in a court of the United States is allowed at the interest rate authorized by law.

2. When a petition for a writ of certiorari, an appeal, or an application for other relief is frivolous, the Court may award the respondent or appellee just damages, and single or double costs under Rule 43. Damages or costs may be awarded against the petitioner, appellant, or applicant, against the party's counsel, or against both party and counsel.

Rule 43. Costs

1. If the Court affirms a judgment, the petitioner or appellant shall pay costs unless the Court otherwise orders.

2. If the Court reverses or vacates a judgment, the respondent or appellee shall pay costs unless the Court otherwise orders.

3. The Clerk's fees and the cost of printing the joint appendix are the only taxable items in this Court. The cost of the transcript of the record from the court below is also a taxable item, but shall be taxable in that court as costs in the case. The expenses of printing briefs, motions, petitions, or jurisdictional statements are not taxable.

4. In a case involving a certified question, costs are equally divided unless the Court otherwise orders, except that if the Court decides the whole matter in controversy, as permitted by Rule 19.2, costs are allowed as provided in paragraphs 1 and 2 of this Rule.

5. To the extent permitted by 28 U.S.C. § 2412, costs under this Rule are allowed for or against the United States or an officer or agent thereof, unless expressly waived or unless the Court otherwise orders.

6. When costs are allowed in this Court, the Clerk will insert an itemization of the costs in the body of the mandate or

judgment sent to the court below. The prevailing side may not submit a bill of costs.

7. In extraordinary circumstances the Court may adjudge double costs.

Rule 44. Rehearing

1. Any petition for the rehearing of any judgment or decision of the Court on the merits shall be filed within 25 days after entry of the judgment or decision, unless the Court or a Justice shortens or extends the time. The petitioner shall file 40 copies of the rehearing petition and shall pay the filing fee prescribed by Rule 38(b), except that a petitioner proceeding *in forma pauperis* under Rule 39, including an inmate of an institution, shall file the number of copies required for a petition by such a person under Rule 12.2. The petition shall state its grounds briefly and distinctly and shall be served as required by Rule 29. The petition shall be presented together with certification of counsel (or of a party unrepresented by counsel) that it is presented in good faith and not for delay; one copy of the certificate shall bear the signature of counsel (or of a party unrepresented by counsel). A copy of the certificate shall follow and be attached to each copy of the petition. A petition for rehearing is not subject to oral argument and will not be granted except by a majority of the Court, at the instance of a Justice who concurred in the judgment or decision.

2. Any petition for the rehearing of an order denying a petition for a writ of certiorari or extraordinary writ shall be filed within 25 days after the date of the order of denial and shall comply with all the form and filing requirements of paragraph 1 of this Rule, including the payment of the filing fee if required, but its grounds shall be limited to intervening circumstances of a substantial or controlling effect or to other substantial grounds not previously presented. The petition shall be presented together with certification of counsel (or of a party unrepresented by counsel) that it is restricted to the grounds specified in this paragraph and that it is presented in

good faith and not for delay; one copy of the certificate shall bear the signature of counsel (or of a party unrepresented by counsel). A copy of the certificate shall follow and be attached to each copy of the petition. The Clerk will not file a petition without a certificate. The petition is not subject to oral argument.

3. The Clerk will not file any response to a petition for rehearing unless the Court requests a response. In the absence of extraordinary circumstances, the Court will not grant a petition for rehearing without first requesting a response.

4. The Clerk will not file consecutive petitions and petitions that are out of time under this Rule.

5. The Clerk will not file any brief for an *amicus curiae* in support of, or in opposition to, a petition for rehearing.

Rule 45. Process; Mandates

1. All process of this Court issues in the name of the President of the United States.

2. In a case on review from a state court, the mandate issues 25 days after entry of the judgment, unless the Court or a Justice shortens or extends the time, or unless the parties stipulate that it issue sooner. The filing of a petition for rehearing stays the mandate until disposition of the petition, unless the Court orders otherwise. If the petition is denied, the mandate issues forthwith.

3. In a case on review from any court of the United States, as defined by 28 U.S.C. § 451, a formal mandate does not issue unless specially directed; instead, the Clerk of this Court will send the clerk of the lower court a copy of the opinion or order of this Court and a certified copy of the judgment. The certified copy of the judgment, prepared and signed by this Court's Clerk, will provide for costs if any are awarded. In all other respects, the provisions of paragraph 2 of this Rule apply.

Rule 46. Dismissing Cases

1. At any stage of the proceedings, whenever all parties file with the Clerk an agreement in writing that a case be dismissed, specifying the terms for payment of costs, and pay to the Clerk any fees then due, the Clerk, without further reference to the Court, will enter an order of dismissal.

2.   (a) A petitioner or appellant may file a motion to dismiss the case, with proof of service as required by Rule 29, tendering to the Clerk any fees due and costs payable. No more than 15 days after service thereof, an adverse party may file an objection, limited to the amount of damages and costs in this Court alleged to be payable or to showing that the moving party does not represent all petitioners or appellants. The Clerk will not file any objection not so limited.

   (b) When the objection asserts that the moving party does not represent all the petitioners or appellants, the party moving for dismissal may file a reply within 10 days, after which time the matter will be submitted to the Court for its determination.

   (c) If no objection is filed—or if upon objection going only to the amount of damages and costs in this Court, the party moving for dismissal tenders the additional damages and costs in full within 10 days of the demand therefor—the Clerk, without further reference to the Court, will enter an order of dismissal. If, after objection as to the amount of damages and costs in this Court, the moving party does not respond by a tender within 10 days, the Clerk will report the matter to the Court for its determination.

3. No mandate or other process will issue on a dismissal under this Rule without an order of the Court.

Part IX. Definitions and Effective Date
Rule 47. Reference to "State Court"; and "State Law"

The term "state court," when used in these Rules, includes the District of Columbia Court of Appeals and the Supreme Court of the Commonwealth of Puerto Rico. See 28 U.S.C. §§ 1257 and 1258. References in these Rules to the common law and statutes of a State include the common law and statutes of the District of Columbia and of the Commonwealth of Puerto Rico.

Rule 48. Effective Date of Rules

1. These Rules, adopted July 26, 1995, will be effective October 2, 1995.
2. The Rules govern all proceedings after their effective date except to the extent that, in the opinion of the Court, their application to a pending matter would not be feasible or would work an injustice, in which event the former procedure applies.

Appendix D:
The United States
Constitution

WHERE THE CONSTITUTION AFFECTS EVERYDAY LIFE

There is no "official" version of the Constitution, so some stylistic liberties have been taken in this reprinting. For example, the word "Clause" along with a number is used here for easier lookup. Also, the twenty-seven amendments are titled "Amendment" rather than the often used "Article."

A few things to bear in mind:

- Although it is not prefaced by the word "Preamble," the opening paragraph is indeed the Preamble.
- Material that has been amended is placed between brackets [ ] and footnoted.
- The first ten amendments are referred to as the Bill of Rights. They were proposed by Congress on September 25, 1789, and ratified on December 15, 1791.
- Beginning with Amendment XI, the date an amendment was proposed and the date it was ratified appear in italics at the beginning of each amendment.

The United States Constitution

We the People of the United States, in Order to form a more perfect Union, establish Justice, insure domestic Tranquility, provide for the common defence, promote the general Welfare, and secure the Blessings of Liberty to ourselves and our Posterity, do ordain and establish this Constitution for the United States of America.

Article I
Section 1

All legislative Powers herein granted shall be vested in a Congress of the United States, which shall consist of a Senate and House of Representatives.

Section 2

Clause 1: The House of Representatives shall be composed of Members chosen every second Year by the People of the several States, and the Electors in each State shall have the Qualifications requisite for Electors of the most numerous Branch of the State Legislature.

Clause 2: No Person shall be a Representative who shall not have attained to the Age of twenty-five Years, and been seven

Years a Citizen of the United States, and who shall not, when elected, be an Inhabitant of that State in which he shall be chosen.

Clause 3: Representatives and [direct Taxes] shall be apportioned among the several States which may be included within this Union, according to their respective Numbers, [which shall be determined by adding to the whole Number of free Persons, including those bound to Service for a Term of Years, and excluding Indians not taxed, three fifths of all other Persons.[1]] The actual Enumeration shall be made within three Years after the first Meeting of the Congress of the United States, and within every subsequent Term of ten Years, in such Manner as they shall by Law direct. The Number of Representatives shall not exceed one for every thirty Thousand, but each State shall have at Least one Representative; and until such enumeration shall be made, the State of New Hampshire shall be entitled to chuse three, Massachusetts eight, Rhode-Island and Providence Plantations one, Connecticut five, New York six, New Jersey four, Pennsylvania eight, Delaware one, Maryland six, Virginia ten, North Carolina five, South Carolina five, and Georgia three.

Clause 4: When vacancies happen in the Representation from any State, the Executive Authority thereof shall issue Writs of Election to fill such Vacancies.

Clause 5: The House of Representatives shall chuse their Speaker and other Officers; and shall have the sole Power of Impeachment.

Section 3

Clause 1: The Senate of the United States shall be composed of two Senators from each State, [chosen by the Legislature thereof,[2]] for six Years; and each Senator shall have one Vote.

Clause 2: Immediately after they shall be assembled in Consequence of the first Election, they shall be divided as equally as may be into three Classes. The Seats of the Senators of the first

Class shall be vacated at the Expiration of the second Year, of the second Class at the Expiration of the fourth Year, and of the third Class at the Expiration of the sixth Year, so that one third may be chosen every second Year; [and if Vacancies happen by Resignation, or otherwise, during the Recess of the Legislature of any State, the Executive thereof may make temporary Appointments until the next Meeting of the Legislature, which shall then fill such Vacancies.[3]]

Clause 3: No Person shall be a Senator who shall not have attained to the Age of thirty Years, and been nine Years a Citizen of the United States, and who shall not, when elected, be an Inhabitant of that State for which he shall be chosen.

Clause 4: The Vice President of the United States shall be President of the Senate, but shall have no Vote, unless they be equally divided.

Clause 5: The Senate shall chuse their other Officers, and also a President pro tempore, in the Absence of the Vice President, or when he shall exercise the Office of President of the United States.

Clause 6: The Senate shall have the sole Power to try all Impeachments. When sitting for that Purpose, they shall be on Oath or Affirmation. When the President of the United States is tried, the Chief Justice shall preside: And no Person shall be convicted without the Concurrence of two thirds of the Members present.

Clause 7: Judgment in Cases of Impeachment shall not extend further than to removal from Office, and disqualification to hold and enjoy any Office of honor, Trust or Profit under the United States: but the Party convicted shall nevertheless be liable and subject to Indictment, Trial, Judgment and Punishment, according to Law.

Section 4

Clause 1: The Times, Places and Manner of holding Elections for Senators and Representatives, shall be prescribed in each State by the Legislature thereof; but the Congress may at any time by Law make or alter such Regulations, except as to the Places of chusing Senators.

Clause 2: The Congress shall assemble at least once in every Year, and such Meeting shall [be on the first Monday in December,[4]] unless they shall by Law appoint a different Day.

Section 5

Clause 1: Each House shall be the Judge of the Elections, Returns and Qualifications of its own Members, and a Majority of each shall constitute a Quorum to do Business; but a smaller Number may adjourn from day to day, and may be authorized to compel the Attendance of absent Members, in such Manner, and under such Penalties as each House may provide.

Clause 2: Each House may determine the Rules of its Proceedings, punish its Members for disorderly Behaviour, and, with the Concurrence of two thirds, expel a Member.

Clause 3: Each House shall keep a Journal of its Proceedings, and from time to time publish the same, excepting such Parts as may in their Judgment require Secrecy; and the Yeas and Nays of the Members of either House on any question shall, at the Desire of one fifth of those Present, be entered on the Journal.

Clause 4: Neither House, during the Session of Congress, shall, without the Consent of the other, adjourn for more than three days, nor to any other Place than that in which the two Houses shall be sitting.

Section 6

Clause 1: [The Senators and Representatives shall receive a Compensation for their Services, to be ascertained by Law, and paid out of the Treasury of the United States.[5]] They shall in all

Cases, except Treason, Felony and Breach of the Peace, be privileged from Arrest during their Attendance at the Session of their respective Houses, and in going to and returning from the same; and for any Speech or Debate in either House, they shall not be questioned in any other Place.

Clause 2: No Senator or Representative shall, during the Time for which he was elected, be appointed to any civil Office under the Authority of the United States, which shall have been created, or the Emoluments whereof shall have been encreased during such time; and no Person holding any Office under the United States, shall be a Member of either House during his Continuance in Office.

Section 7
Clause 1: All Bills for raising Revenue shall originate in the House of Representatives; but the Senate may propose or concur with Amendments as on other Bills.

Clause 2: Every Bill which shall have passed the House of Representatives and the Senate, shall, before it become a Law, be presented to the President of the United States; If he approve he shall sign it, but if not he shall return it, with his Objections to that House in which it shall have originated, who shall enter the Objections at large on their Journal, and proceed to reconsider it. If after such Reconsideration two thirds of that House shall agree to pass the Bill, it shall be sent, together with the Objections, to the other House, by which it shall likewise be reconsidered, and if approved by two thirds of that House, it shall become a Law. But in all such Cases the Votes of both Houses shall be determined by Yeas and Nays, and the Names of the Persons voting for and against the Bill shall be entered on the Journal of each House respectively. If any Bill shall not be returned by the President within ten Days (Sundays excepted) after it shall have been presented to him, the Same shall be a Law, in like Manner as if he had signed it, unless the Congress by their Adjournment prevent its Return, in which Case it shall not be a Law.

Clause 3: Every Order, Resolution, or Vote to which the Concurrence of the Senate and House of Representatives may be necessary (except on a question of Adjournment) shall be presented to the President of the United States; and before the Same shall take Effect, shall be approved by him, or being disapproved by him, shall be repassed by two thirds of the Senate and House of Representatives, according to the Rules and Limitations prescribed in the Case of a Bill.

Section 8

Clause 1: The Congress shall have Power To lay and collect Taxes, Duties, Imposts and Excises, to pay the Debts and provide for the common Defence and general Welfare of the United States; but all Duties, Imposts and Excises shall be uniform throughout the United States;

Clause 2: To borrow Money on the credit of the United States;

Clause 3: To regulate Commerce with foreign Nations, and among the several States, and with the Indian Tribes;

Clause 4: To establish an uniform Rule of Naturalization, and uniform Laws on the subject of Bankruptcies throughout the United States;

Clause 5: To coin Money, regulate the Value thereof, and of foreign Coin, and fix the Standard of Weights and Measures;

Clause 6: To provide for the Punishment of counterfeiting the Securities and current Coin of the United States;

Clause 7: To establish Post Offices and post Roads;

Clause 8: To promote the Progress of Science and useful Arts, by securing for limited Times to Authors and Inventors the exclusive Right to their respective Writings and Discoveries;

Clause 9: To constitute Tribunals inferior to the supreme Court;

Clause 10: To define and punish Piracies and Felonies committed on the high Seas, and Offences against the Law of Nations;

Clause 11: To declare War, grant Letters of Marque and Reprisal, and make Rules concerning Captures on Land and Water;

Clause 12: To raise and support Armies, but no Appropriation of Money to that Use shall be for a longer Term than two Years;

Clause 13: To provide and maintain a Navy;

Clause 14: To make Rules for the Government and Regulation of the land and naval Forces;

Clause 15: To provide for calling forth the Militia to execute the Laws of the Union, suppress Insurrections and repel Invasions;

Clause 16: To provide for organizing, arming, and disciplining, the Militia, and for governing such Part of them as may be employed in the Service of the United States, reserving to the States respectively, the Appointment of the Officers, and the Authority of training the Militia according to the discipline prescribed by Congress;

Clause 17: To exercise exclusive Legislation in all Cases whatsoever, over such District (not exceeding ten Miles square) as may, by Cession of particular States, and the Acceptance of Congress, become the Seat of the Government of the United States, and to exercise like Authority over all Places purchased by the Consent of the Legislature of the State in which the Same shall be, for the Erection of Forts, Magazines, Arsenals, dock-Yards, and other needful Buildings;—And

Clause 18: To make all Laws which shall be necessary and proper for carrying into Execution the foregoing Powers, and all other Powers vested by this Constitution in the Government of the United States, or in any Department or Officer thereof.

Section 9

Clause 1: The Migration or Importation of such Persons as any of the States now existing shall think proper to admit, shall not be prohibited by the Congress prior to the Year one thousand eight hundred and eight, but a Tax or duty may be imposed on such Importation, not exceeding ten dollars for each Person.

Clause 2: The Privilege of the Writ of Habeas Corpus shall not be suspended, unless when in Cases of Rebellion or Invasion the public Safety may require it.

Clause 3: No Bill of Attainder or ex post facto Law shall be passed.

Clause 4: [No Capitation, or other direct, Tax shall be laid, unless in Proportion to the Census or Enumeration herein before directed to be taken.[6]]

Clause 5: No Tax or Duty shall be laid on Articles exported from any State.

Clause 6: No Preference shall be given by any Regulation of Commerce or Revenue to the Ports of one State over those of another: nor shall Vessels bound to, or from, one State, be obliged to enter, clear, or pay Duties in another.

Clause 7: No Money shall be drawn from the Treasury, but in Consequence of Appropriations made by Law; and a regular Statement and Account of the Receipts and Expenditures of all public Money shall be published from time to time.

Clause 8: No Title of Nobility shall be granted by the United States: And no Person holding any Office of Profit or Trust under them, shall, without the Consent of the Congress, accept of any present, Emolument, Office, or Title, of any kind whatever, from any King, Prince, or foreign State.

Section 10

Clause 1: No State shall enter into any Treaty, Alliance, or Confederation; grant Letters of Marque and Reprisal; coin Money; emit Bills of Credit; make any Thing but gold and silver Coin a Tender in Payment of Debts; pass any Bill of Attainder, ex post facto Law, or Law impairing the Obligation of Contracts, or grant any Title of Nobility.

Clause 2: No State shall, without the Consent of the Congress, lay any Imposts or Duties on Imports or Exports, except what may be absolutely necessary for executing its inspection Laws: and the net Produce of all Duties and Imposts, laid by any State on Imports or Exports, shall be for the Use of the Treasury of the United States; and all such Laws shall be subject to the Revision and Controul of the Congress.

Clause 3: No State shall, without the Consent of Congress, lay any Duty of Tonnage, keep Troops, or Ships of War in time of Peace, enter into any Agreement or Compact with another State, or with a foreign Power, or engage in War, unless actually invaded, or in such imminent Danger as will not admit of delay.

Article II
Section 1

Clause 1: The executive Power shall be vested in a President of the United States of America. He shall hold his Office during the Term of four Years, and, together with the Vice President, chosen for the same Term, be elected, as follows.

Clause 2: Each State shall appoint, in such Manner as the Legislature thereof may direct, a Number of Electors, equal to the whole Number of Senators and Representatives to which the State may be entitled in the Congress: but no Senator or Representative, or Person holding an Office of Trust or Profit under the United States, shall be appointed an Elector.

Appointments are not herein otherwise provided for, and which shall be established by Law: but the Congress may by Law vest the Appointment of such inferior Officers, as they think proper, in the President alone, in the Courts of Law, or in the Heads of Departments.

Clause 3: The President shall have Power to fill up all Vacancies that may happen during the Recess of the Senate, by granting Commissions which shall expire at the End of their next Session.

Section 3
He shall from time to time give to the Congress Information of the State of the Union, and recommend to their Consideration such Measures as he shall judge necessary and expedient; he may, on extraordinary Occasions, convene both Houses, or either of them, and in Case of Disagreement between them, with Respect to the Time of Adjournment, he may adjourn them to such Time as he shall think proper; he shall receive Ambassadors and other public Ministers; he shall take Care that the Laws be faithfully executed, and shall Commission all the Officers of the United States.

Section 4
The President, Vice President and all civil Officers of the United States, shall be removed from Office on Impeachment for, and Conviction of, Treason, Bribery, or other high Crimes and Misdemeanors.

Article III
Section 1
The judicial Power of the United States, shall be vested in one supreme Court, and in such inferior Courts as the Congress may from time to time ordain and establish. The Judges, both of the supreme and inferior Courts, shall hold their Offices during good Behaviour, and shall, at stated Times, receive for their Services, a Compensation, which shall not be diminished during their Continuance in Office.

New Hampshire

John Langdon
Nicholas Gilman

Massachusetts

Nathaniel Gorham
Rufus King

Connecticut

WM. SamL. Johnson
Roger Sherman

New Jersey

Wil. Livingston
David Brearley
WM. Paterson
Jona. Dayton

Pennsylvania
B. Franklin
Thomas Mifflin
Rob T Morris
Geo. Clymer
ThoS. FitzSimons
Jared Ingersoll
James Wilson
Gouv Morris

New York

Alexander Hamilton

Attest William Jackson
Secretary

Amendments to the Constitution

Amendment I
Congress shall make no law respecting an establishment of religion, or prohibiting the free exercise thereof; or abridging the freedom of speech, or of the press; or the right of the people peaceably to assemble, and to petition the Government for a redress of grievances.

Amendment II
A well regulated Militia, being necessary to the security of a free State, the right of the people to keep and bear Arms, shall not be infringed.

Amendment III

No Soldier shall, in time of peace be quartered in any house, without the consent of the Owner, nor in time of war, but in a manner to be prescribed by law.

Amendment IV

The right of the people to be secure in their persons, houses, papers, and effects, against unreasonable searches and seizures, shall not be violated, and no Warrants shall issue, but upon probable cause, supported by Oath or affirmation, and particularly describing the place to be searched, and the persons or things to be seized.

Amendment V

No person shall be held to answer for a capital, or otherwise infamous crime, unless on a presentment or indictment of a Grand Jury, except in cases arising in the land or naval forces, or in the Militia, when in actual service in time of War or public danger; nor shall any person be subject for the same offence to be twice put in jeopardy of life or limb; nor shall be compelled in any criminal case to be a witness against himself, nor be deprived of life, liberty, or property, without due process of law; nor shall private property be taken for public use, without just compensation.

Amendment VI

In all criminal prosecutions, the accused shall enjoy the right to a speedy and public trial, by an impartial jury of the State and district wherein the crime shall have been committed, which district shall have been previously ascertained by law, and to be informed of the nature and cause of the accusation; to be confronted with the witnesses against him; to have compulsory process for obtaining witnesses in his favor, and to have the Assistance of Counsel for his defence.

Amendment VII

In Suits at common law, where the value in controversy shall exceed twenty dollars, the right of trial by jury shall be preserved, and no fact tried by a jury, shall be otherwise re-examined in any Court of the United States, than according to the rules of the common law.

Amendment VIII

Excessive bail shall not be required, nor excessive fines imposed, nor cruel and unusual punishments inflicted.

Amendment IX

The enumeration in the Constitution, of certain rights, shall not be construed to deny or disparage others retained by the people.

Amendment X

The powers not delegated to the United States by the Constitution, nor prohibited by it to the States, are reserved to the States respectively, or to the people.

Amendment XI

(Proposed March 4, 1794; ratified February 7, 1795.) The Judicial power of the United States shall not be construed to extend to any suit in law or equity, commenced or prosecuted against one of the United States by Citizens of another State, or by Citizens or Subjects of any Foreign State.

Amendment XII

(Proposed December 9, 1803; ratified June 15, 1804.) The Electors shall meet in their respective states, and vote by ballot for President and Vice-President, one of whom, at least, shall not be an inhabitant of the same state with themselves; they shall name in their ballots the person voted for as President, and in distinct ballots the person voted for as Vice-President, and they shall make distinct lists of all persons voted for as President, and of all persons voted for as Vice-President, and of the number of votes for each, which lists they shall sign and certify, and transmit sealed to the seat of the government of the United States, directed to the President of the Senate;—The President of the Senate shall, in the presence of the Senate and House of Representatives, open all the certificates and the votes shall then be

counted;—The person having the greatest number of votes for President, shall be the President, if such number be a majority of the whole number of Electors appointed; and if no person have such majority, then from the persons having the highest numbers not exceeding three on the list of those voted for as President, the House of Representatives shall choose immediately, by ballot, the President. But in choosing the President, the votes shall be taken by states, the representation from each state having one vote; a quorum for this purpose shall consist of a member or members from two-thirds of the states, and a majority of all the states shall be necessary to a choice. And if the House of Representatives shall not choose a President whenever the right of choice shall devolve upon them, before [the fourth day of March next following, then the Vice-President shall act as President, as in the case of the death or other constitutional disability of the President.[11]]—The person having the greatest number of votes as Vice-President, shall be the Vice-President, if such number be a majority of the whole number of Electors appointed, and if no person have a majority, then from the two highest numbers on the list, the Senate shall choose the Vice-President; a quorum for the purpose shall consist of two-thirds of the whole number of Senators, and a majority of the whole number shall be necessary to a choice. But no person constitutionally ineligible to the office of President shall be eligible to that of Vice-President of the United States.

Amendment XIII
(Proposed January 31, 1865; ratified December 6, 1865.)

Section 1
Neither slavery nor involuntary servitude, except as a punishment for crime whereof the party shall have been duly convicted, shall exist within the United States, or any place subject to their jurisdiction.

Section 2
Congress shall have power to enforce this article by appropriate legislation.

Amendment XIV
(Proposed June 13, 1866; ratified July 9, 1868.)

Section 1

All persons born or naturalized in the United States, and subject to the jurisdiction thereof, are citizens of the United States and of the State wherein they reside. No State shall make or enforce any law which shall abridge the privileges or immunities of citizens of the United States; nor shall any State deprive any person of life, liberty, or property, without due process of law; nor deny to any person within its jurisdiction the equal protection of the laws.

Section 2

Representatives shall be apportioned among the several States according to their respective numbers, counting the whole number of persons in each State, excluding Indians not taxed. But when the right to vote at any election for the choice of electors for President and Vice President of the United States, Representatives in Congress, the Executive and Judicial officers of a State, or the members of the Legislature thereof, is denied to any of the male inhabitants of such State, [being twenty-one years of age,[12]] and citizens of the United States, or in any way abridged, except for participation in rebellion, or other crime, the basis of representation therein shall be reduced in the proportion which the number of such male citizens shall bear to the whole number of male citizens twenty-one years of age in such State.

Section 3

No person shall be a Senator or Representative in Congress, or elector of President and Vice President, or hold any office, civil or military, under the United States, or under any State, who, having previously taken an oath, as a member of Congress, or as an officer of the United States, or as a member of any State legislature, or as an executive or judicial officer of any State, to support the Constitution of the United States, shall have engaged in insurrection or rebellion against the same, or given aid or comfort to the enemies thereof. But Congress may by a vote of two-thirds of each House, remove such disability.

Section 4

The validity of the public debt of the United States, authorized by law, including debts incurred for payment of pensions and bounties for services in suppressing insurrection or rebellion, shall not be questioned. But neither the United States nor any State shall assume or pay any debt or obligation incurred in aid of insurrection or rebellion against the United States, or any claim for the loss or emancipation of any slave; but all such debts, obligations and claims shall be held illegal and void.

Section 5

The Congress shall have power to enforce, by appropriate legislation, the provisions of this article.

Amendment XV

(Proposed February 26, 1869; ratified February 3, 1870.)

Section 1

The right of citizens of the United States to vote shall not be denied or abridged by the United States or by any State on account of race, color, or previous condition of servitude.

Section 2

The Congress shall have power to enforce this article by appropriate legislation.

Amendment XVI

(Proposed July 12, 1909; ratified February 3, 1913.) The Congress shall have power to lay and collect taxes on incomes, from whatever source derived, without apportionment among the several States, and without regard to any census or enumeration.

Amendment XVII

(Proposed May 13, 1912; ratified April 8, 1913.) The Senate of the United States shall be composed of two Senators from each

State, elected by the people thereof, for six years; and each Senator shall have one vote. The electors in each State shall have the qualifications requisite for electors of the most numerous branch of the State legislatures.

When vacancies happen in the representation of any State in the Senate, the executive authority of such State shall issue writs of election to fill such vacancies: *Provided,* That the legislature of any State may empower the executive thereof to make temporary appointments until the people fill the vacancies by election as the legislature may direct.

This amendment shall not be so construed as to affect the election or term of any Senator chosen before it becomes valid as part of the Constitution.

Amendment XVIII
(Proposed December 18, 1917; ratified January 16, 1919.)

[Section 1
After one year from the ratification of this article the manufacture, sale, or transportation of intoxicating liquors within, the importation thereof into, or the exportation thereof from the United States and all territory subject to the jurisdiction thereof for beverage purposes is hereby prohibited.

Section 2
The Congress and the several States shall have concurrent power to enforce this article by appropriate legislation.

Section 3
This article shall be inoperative unless it shall have been ratified as an amendment to the Constitution by the legislatures of the several States, as provided in the Constitution, within seven years from the date of the submission hereof to the States by the Congress.[13]]

Amendment XIX

(Proposed June 4, 1919; ratified August 18, 1920.) The right of citizens of the United States to vote shall not be denied or abridged by the United States or by any State on account of sex.

Congress shall have power to enforce this article by appropriate legislation.

Amendment XX

(Proposed March 2, 1932; ratified January 23, 1933.)

Section 1

The terms of the President and Vice President shall end at noon on the 20th day of January, and the terms of Senators and Representatives at noon on the 3d day of January, of the years in which such terms would have ended if this article had not been ratified; and the terms of their successors shall then begin.

Section 2

The Congress shall assemble at least once in every year, and such meeting shall begin at noon on the 3d day of January, unless they shall by law appoint a different day.

Section 3

If, at the time fixed for the beginning of the term of the President, the President elect shall have died, the Vice President elect shall become President. If a President shall not have been chosen before the time fixed for the beginning of his term, or if the President elect shall have failed to qualify, then the Vice President elect shall act as President until a President shall have qualified; and the Congress may by law provide for the case wherein neither a President elect nor a Vice President elect shall have qualified, declaring who shall then act as President, or the manner in which one who is to act shall be selected, and such person shall act accordingly until a President or Vice President shall have qualified.

Section 4
The Congress may by law provide for the case of the death of any of the persons from whom the House of Representatives may choose a President whenever the right of choice shall have devolved upon them, and for the case of the death of any of the persons from whom the Senate may choose a Vice President whenever the right of choice shall have devolved upon them.

Section 5
Sections 1 and 2 shall take effect on the 15th day of October following the ratification of this article.

Section 6
This article shall be inoperative unless it shall have been ratified as an amendment to the Constitution by the legislatures of three-fourths of the several States within seven years from the date of its submission.

Amendment XXI
(Proposed February 20, 1933; ratified December 5, 1933.)

Section 1
The eighteenth article of amendment to the Constitution of the United States is hereby repealed.

Section 2
The transportation or importation into any State, Territory, or possession of the United States for delivery or use therein of intoxicating liquors, in violation of the laws thereof, is hereby prohibited.

Section 3
This article shall be inoperative unless it shall have been ratified as an amendment to the Constitution by conventions in the several States, as provided in the Constitution, within seven years from the date of the submission hereof to the States by the Congress.

Amendment XXII
(Proposed March 21, 1947, ratified February 27, 1951.)

Section 1

No person shall be elected to the office of the President more than twice, and no person who has held the office of President, or acted as President, for more than two years of a term to which some other person was elected President shall be elected to the office of the President more than once. But this Article shall not apply to any person holding the office of President when this Article was proposed by the Congress, and shall not prevent any person who may be holding the office of President, or acting as President, during the term within which this Article becomes operative from holding the office of President or acting as President during the remainder of such term.

Section 2

This article shall be inoperative unless it shall have been ratified as an amendment to the Constitution by the legislatures of three-fourths of the several States within seven years from the date of its submission to the States by the Congress.

Amendment XXIII
(Proposed June 16, 1960; ratified March 29, 1961.)

Section 1

The District constituting the seat of Government of the United States shall appoint in such manner as the Congress may direct:

A number of electors of President and Vice President equal to the whole number of Senators and Representatives in Congress to which the District would be entitled if it were a State, but in no event more than the least populous State; they shall be in addition to those appointed by the States, but they shall be considered, for the purposes of the election of President and Vice President, to be electors appointed by a State; and they shall meet in the District and perform such duties as provided by the twelfth article of amendment.

Section 2

The Congress shall have power to enforce this article by appropriate legislation.

Amendment XXIV
(Proposed August 27, 1962; ratified January 23, 1964.)

Section 1

The right of citizens of the United States to vote in any primary or other election for President or Vice President, for electors for President or Vice President, or for Senator or Representative in Congress, shall not be denied or abridged by the United States or any State by reason of failure to pay any poll tax or other tax.

Section 2

The Congress shall have power to enforce this article by appropriate legislation.

Amendment XXV
(Proposed July 6, 1965; ratified February 10, 1967.)

Section 1

In case of the removal of the President from office or of his death or resignation, the Vice President shall become President.

Section 2

Whenever there is a vacancy in the office of the Vice President, the President shall nominate a Vice President who shall take office upon confirmation by a majority vote of both Houses of Congress.

Section 3

Whenever the President transmits to the President pro tempore of the Senate and the Speaker of the House of Representatives his written declaration that he is unable to discharge the powers and duties of his office, and until he transmits to them a written declaration to the contrary, such powers and duties shall be discharged by the Vice President as Acting President.

Section 4

Whenever the Vice President and a majority of either the principal officers of the executive departments or of such other body as Congress may by law provide, transmit to the President pro tempore of the Senate and the Speaker of the House of Representatives their written declaration that the President is unable to discharge the powers and duties of his office, the Vice President shall immediately assume the powers and duties of the office as Acting President.

Thereafter, when the President transmits to the President pro tempore of the Senate and the Speaker of the House of Representatives his written declaration that no inability exists, he shall resume the powers and duties of his office unless the Vice President and a majority of either the principal officers of the executive department or of such other body as Congress may by law provide, transmit within four days to the President pro tempore of the Senate and the Speaker of the House of Representatives their written declaration that the President is unable to discharge the powers and duties of his office. Thereupon Congress shall decide the issue, assembling within forty-eight hours for that purpose if not in session. If the Congress, within twenty-one days after receipt of the latter written declaration, or, if Congress is not in session, within twenty-one days after Congress is required to assemble, determines by two-thirds vote of both Houses that the President is unable to discharge the powers and duties of his office, the Vice President shall continue to discharge the same as Acting President; otherwise, the President shall resume the powers and duties of his office.

Amendment XXVI
(Proposed March 23, 1971; ratified July 1, 1971.)

Section 1

The right of citizens of the United States, who are eighteen years of age or older, to vote shall not be denied or abridged by the United States or by any State on account of age.

Section 2

The Congress shall have power to enforce this article by appropriate legislation.

Amendment XXVII.[14]

(Proposed September 25, 1789; ratified May 7, 1992.) No law, varying the compensation for the services of the Senators and Representatives, shall take effect, until an election of Representatives shall have intervened.

Notes

1. The first part of this clause relating to taxes on incomes without apportionment was affected by Amendment XVI. The second part relating to the mode of apportionment of representatives among the several States has been affected by section 2 of Amendment XIV.
2. This Clause has been affected by Clause 1 of Amendment XVII.
3. This Clause has been affected by Clause 2 of Amendment XVII.
4. This Clause has been affected by Amendment XX.
5. This Clause has been affected by Amendment XXVII.
6. This Clause has been affected by Amendment XVI.
7. This Clause has been superseded by Amendment XII.
8. This Clause has been affected by Amendment XXV.
9. This Clause has been affected by Amendment XI.
10. This Clause has been affected by Amendment XIII.
11. This Clause has been superseded by Amendment XX, section 3.
12. This section has been affected by Amendment XXVI, section 1.
13. This Amendment was repealed by Amendment XXI, section 1.
14. This Amendment, being the second of twelve articles proposed by the First Congress on September 25, 1789, was declared by the Archivist of the United States on May 18, 1992, to have been ratified by the legislatures of forty of the fifty States.

Index